Covert Processes at Work

To Hassan,

May all your secret hopes
and dreams come true!
Best Wishes,
Bob Marshak

American University
January 11, 2009

COVERT
Processes
at Work

Managing the Five Hidden Dimensions of Organizational Change

ROBERT J. MARSHAK

BK®

BERRETT-KOEHLER PUBLISHERS, INC.
San Francisco

Berrett-Koehler Publishers, Inc.
235 Montgomery Street, Suite 650
San Francisco, CA 94104-2916
Tel: (415) 288-0260   Fax: (415) 362-2512   www.bkconnection.com

Ordering Information

Quantity sales. Special discounts are available on quantity purchases by corporations, associations, and
others. For details, contact the "Special Sales Department" at the Berrett-Koehler address above.

Individual sales. Berrett-Koehler publications are available through most bookstores. They can also be or-
dered directly from Berrett-Koehler: Tel: (800) 929-2929; Fax: (802) 864-7626; www.bkconnection.com

Orders for college textbook/course adoption use. Please contact Berrett-Koehler: Tel: (800) 929-2929;
Fax: (802) 864-7626.

Orders by U.S. trade bookstores and wholesalers. Please contact Ingram Publisher Services, Tel: (800)
509-4887; Fax: (800) 838-1149; E-mail: customer.service@ingrampublisherservices.com; or visit www.
ingrampublisherservices.com/Ordering for details about electronic ordering.

Berrett-Koehler and the BK logo are registered trademarks of Berrett-Koehler Publishers, Inc. All rights
reserved.

Printed in the United States of America

Berrett-Koehler books are printed on long-lasting acid-free paper. When it is available, we choose paper that has been manufactured by environmentally responsible processes. These may include using trees
grown in sustainable forests, incorporating recycled paper, minimizing chlorine in bleaching, or recycling
the energy produced at the paper mill.

Library of Congress Cataloging-in-Publication Data
Marshak, Robert J., 1946–
Covert processes at work : managing the five hidden dimensions of organizational change / by Robert J.
Marshak
    p.   cm.
Includes bibliographical references and index.
ISBN: 978-1-57675-415-3
1. Organizational change. 2. Organizational change—Management. 3. Organizational behavior. 4. Man-
agement—Psychological aspects. I. Title.
HD58.8M3318 2006
658.4'06—dc22 2006040078

First Edition
12 11 10 09 08   10 9 8 7 6 5 4 3 2

Design and production: Detta Penna
Copyediting: Judith Johnstone
Indexing: Joan Dickey

 *To Allison,*

who helped me see above-the-clouds.

Contents

Foreword   ix
Preface   xi
Acknowledgments   xv

1   Covert Dimensions and Change   1

2   The Covert Processes Model   19

3   Cues and Clues   35

4   Decoding Subconscious Expressions   53

5   Five Basic Keys   69

6   Putting Things On-the-Table   87

7   Recognizing and Rethinking Interventions   105

8   Reframing Interventions   127

9   Rethinking Organizational Politics   143

10 Managing Covert Processes   163

Bibliography of Selected Topics   171
References   177
Index   179
About the Author   187

Foreword

The existence of covert processes has been known for a long time. Whether we called them hidden agendas, unconscious desires, the elephant under-the-table, latent functions, or shared tacit assumptions, we knew they were there but rarely had a clear idea what to do about them.

For the therapist, the challenge has typically been how to bring the covert to the surface in a helpful way. For the group therapist or team leader, the complication was how to make members aware that they not only carried individual hidden agendas but also that the group itself evolved covert assumptions that guided and constrained its behavior to an unknown degree. For the negotiator or diplomat, the existence of covert intentions was taken for granted as intrinsic to the process of reaching agreement; diplomacy lay in knowing how to make the covert known without actually revealing it directly or at the wrong time.

In the human relations and organization development movement, there was a period when "openness" was taken almost as an absolute value—"let it all hang out, it will be good for you." Giving feedback, telling people what we thought of them, was thought to improve relations and task accomplishment. But the introduction of sensitivity training into organizations soon showed that some kinds of openness were not welcome. We discovered that social norms about what to say and not say to each other could not be subverted without some undesirable consequences. Etiquette, tact, and politeness often required keeping covert things covert. But we also knew that covert processes strongly influenced the outcomes of social action, often in a negative way, so we could not simply ignore them.

I mention all of these issues and unresolved dilemmas because in this book we finally have a coherent approach to all of them. Not only does Bob Marshak provide under one cover an inventory of individual, group, and organizational covert processes, but he also provides ways of assessing them and dealing with them. This should be particularly useful to organizational consultants and managers because it makes us realize that in all social interaction there are multiple covert processes operating. How we deal with them will obviously vary with the situation and there are no formulas for dealing with the covert, but if we cannot identify and perceive their operation we cannot deal with them at all. The reader will appreciate the many insights that this book provides.

Edgar H. Schein

▶ Preface

This is a book about powerful processes that impact organizations but usually remain unseen, unspoken, or unacknowledged. Collectively called *covert processes,* they include hidden agendas, blind spots, organizational politics, the elephant in the room, secret hopes and wishes, tacit assumptions, and unconscious dynamics.

Although covert in their workings, these processes can be insidious in their impacts, often shaping outcomes without our fully realizing it. One of my earliest encounters with covert processes at work was during a meeting between the heads of two divisions. The meeting had been called to resolve conflicts over responsibilities and to establish greater collaboration between the two divisions. I was there in a staff role to follow up on any agreements that came out of the discussions. The two division heads greeted each other in friendly terms and exchanged jokes and pleasantries. Eventually they each acknowledged that there were disagreements and difficulties that were creating problems. After about an hour, they smiled at each other, shook hands, and got up to leave. Even though I was not supposed to speak, I blurted out, "But what are you going to do about the issues? You didn't agree to anything." The division heads both looked at me, said nothing, and walked out of the room. After they left, one of the other people in attendance turned to me and said, "They can't stand each other." This may have been one of my earliest encounters with covert processes at work, but it certainly was not my last. In more than thirty years as a staff specialist, executive, and organization change consultant I have witnessed the impacts of many types of covert processes on a daily basis.

Purpose

My experiences with covert processes, especially during organizational change, led me to inquire more deeply into their causes and manifestations and to try out different ways to identify and address them. It also led to developing and facilitating for many years with my colleague Judith H. Katz a training program called the "Dealing with Covert Processes Workshop." During the workshops we had opportunities to work with participants from all types of organizations, and to test and refine our insights and ideas about covert processes. Furthermore, despite the routine warnings in management textbooks that what is overt in organizations is only the tip of the iceberg, I also discovered that with a few exceptions (e.g., Egan, 1994) there was little guidance available on how to deal with the unseen aspects of the iceberg. All of this convinced me that a manual to help change leaders, staff specialists, and consultants better understand, recognize, and manage the covert processes that could undermine their change efforts would be a useful contribution.

In some ways this book can be seen as an extension of the pioneering work by organizational psychologist Ed Schein on process consultation, especially on the importance of being able to decipher hidden forces. "One of the most important functions of process consultation is to make visible that which is invisible" (1999, p. 84). Toward that end, this book provides frameworks, principles, and practices that will be useful in diagnosing and addressing the hidden dynamics that can impact what you are doing and how it gets done. Although the ideas are grounded in a wide range of social science research and theory, there is little attention to definitions and literature reviews of specific theories or types of covert processes. A thematic bibliography is included for readers interested in exploring the ideas that helped shape the book.

Finally, the book integrates all hidden dynamics instead of focusing on one or two. It asks and answers the question: What do all types of covert processes have in common and what can you do about them?

Organization

The book is organized into ten chapters that address both principles and practices. The examples and cases are based on real incidents. Except when referring to the author, the names of companies, individuals, and some information have been disguised.

Chapter 1 addresses the overt and covert dimensions of organizational change and why focusing only on what is overt and rational will be insufficient to ensure success in most change efforts. Five more covert dimensions will need attention to increase the likelihood of success. Separately and together, those dimensions have the potential to block even the best-planned change effort. The Analyteks case illustrates these concepts.

Chapter 2 continues laying the foundation by presenting an integrated framework to explain the sources and manifestations of all covert processes. This framework is called the Covert Processes Model and is based on the metaphor of what's on the table and what's not. This model forms the theoretical foundation for the diagnostic and action principles described later in the book. The model is then applied to understanding the Whiz Tech case.

Chapter 3 is the first of two chapters on diagnosing covert processes—or "how to go about seeing what is not there." It presents and explains a formula for diagnosing covert processes. This formula offers a method for developing hunches about the presence of possible covert dynamics, which is then illustrated through the Alpha Corporation case. The chapter ends with a discussion of diagnosing covert processes in work groups and work teams.

Chapter 4 continues the theme of diagnosis by explaining how intentional and unintentional symbolic communications, such as word images, may reveal important insights for developing hunches about hidden dynamics. The paradoxical principle that you need to "explore symbolic messages literally and literal messages symbolically" is introduced as one way to guide symbolic diagnosis. The chapter illustrates four symbolic modalities and shows how they can help reveal what might otherwise be covert. The Smith-Jones case demonstrates the way symbolic communications serve as early indicators of covert organizational themes.

Chapter 5 begins the active part of the book by presenting five keys to preparing yourself to engage covert processes successfully in pursuit of organizational change. Collectively, the five keys form the "basics" for anyone wishing to address covert dynamics. The chapter concludes by showing how the basics were applied in the Comfort Foods case.

Chapter 6 focuses on how to engage and manage covert dynamics. It illustrates four general approaches with examples. The chapter ends by showing how the approaches were used in the Common Program Structure case.

Chapter 7 presents ways to address hidden beliefs through recognizing and rethinking interventions with specific tools, methodologies, and examples. Chapter 8 concludes the discussion of interventions with an extended discussion of the principles and practices of reframing. Two cases show the practices in action.

Chapter 9 invites you to rethink and reframe your ideas about organizational politics. The chapter posits that there are political and managerial perspectives to organizational change and that it is important to be able to use both to ensure success. The chapter discusses operating from a political perspective and presents a framework for diagnosing an organization's political system. A comparison of the ABC and XYZ Corporations underscores the chapter's ideas.

Chapter 10 summarizes the book by looking at comments and guidelines for addressing covert processes in your organization during organizational change.

Concluding Comments

Over the years, I have found the models, principles, and practices presented in this book to be a powerful framework for addressing covert dynamics that might otherwise impede your change effort. This framework invites you to think and act more holistically and to consider possibilities that traditional change practices may downplay or ignore. This book will help you to address the literal and the symbolic; the conscious and the unconscious; the rational and the artistic; deep fears and great hopes; what is said and done, and what is not spoken and suppressed. Use the information wisely, ethically, and for the purpose of enhancing the performance of individuals, groups and organizations.

Robert J. Marshak
Reston, Virginia
January 2006

Acknowledgments

Although writing is often an individual process, there are many people who overtly and covertly helped make this book possible. I am especially appreciative of my colleagues, mentors, clients, and workshop participants who have contributed to the ideas, theories, and experiences that led to the creation of this book.

First, and foremost, I'd like to thank my colleague and friend, Judith H. Katz. This book would not have been possible without her. From the beginning, Judith was involved in our joint exploration of the world of covert processes. She co-created the Covert Processes Model, the framework we developed to organize our thoughts and actions about covert processes, and she was a full collaborator in developing ideas, approaches, and interventions. Judith has been a wonderfully supportive colleague throughout our many years together as designers and facilitators of the "Dealing with Covert Processes Workshop," and throughout the writing of this book. Judith, an overt and public thank you!

I also wish to acknowledge and thank my wife, Allison Binder Marshak. Allison introduced me to transpersonal psychology and Psychosynthesis. She also suggested to Judith and me that, in addition to what was on-the-table and under-the-table, we needed to consider what was hidden above-the-clouds. This idea transformed the way we conceived of covert processes and was quickly incorporated into the final framework. Allison has been very supportive in getting this book written and has been a source of constant encouragement to me.

Many colleagues and mentors have supported my writing or contributed significantly to my thinking about organizations, organizational change, and hidden dynamics. These include Morely Segal, Bob Boynton, and Don Zauderer, who guided my graduate studies and exposed me to the complexities and politics of organizations in theory; Len Covello and Ernie Corley, who were my bosses during my years in public service and taught me about the complexities and politics of organizations in practice; and Don Klein, Edie Seashore, Darya Funches, Charlie Seashore, and Brenda B. Jones, who have been mentors or colleagues for many years and have always been supportive of my endeavors. I also wish to thank Cyndi Harris, who recently joined me in co-facilitating the "Dealing with Covert Processes Workshop" after Judith moved on. Without Cyndi's support, energy, and enthusiasm this whole project may have come to an end several years ago.

In a special acknowledgement, I'd like to thank overtly the many unnamed people who helped make this book possible by privately supporting me, working behind the scenes, contributing early anonymous reviews of the manuscript, and so much more. I'd also like to thank all those who participated in workshops facilitated by Judith, Cyndi, and me. We learned so much from your willingness to explore covert processes with us, and your responses and reactions helped to validate or modify our thinking.

Finally, the people at Berrett-Koehler Publishers deserve a heartfelt thank you for their attentive support and professionalism throughout the publishing process. From my initial phone call to Johanna Vondeling through the last days of proofing and thinking about marketing, everyone at Berrett-Koehler was responsive and attentive to my needs and ambitions for the book.

CHAPTER 1

Covert Dimensions and Change

Have you ever sat through a business meeting, thinking "Something is going on here that is really getting in the way, but I can't put my finger on it." You were probably sensing covert processes at work. Covert processes are hidden dynamics that routinely impact human interactions and can confound our most diligent efforts to accomplish our goals. When we try to effect organizational change, these hidden factors impact our ability to recognize the need for change, plan appropriate responses, align people and resources, and successfully implement new initiatives. In short, covert processes are a crucial aspect of organizational change and, when not made explicit, they can block even the best of intentions.

The term *covert processes* is used here to mean any hidden or unconscious dynamic. In every culture there are unspoken beliefs and assumptions underlying people's behavior. They affect what we say and do even though we may not be aware of them. From a psychological viewpoint, covert processes include the unspoken mental models and unconscious dynamics of individuals and groups. In everyday usage, the term *covert* tends to evoke images of spies, intrigue, and secret deals. For our purposes we define *covert* more neutrally as "out-of-everyday awareness." Covert processes include all out-of-awareness dynamics that occur in human systems, for whatever reasons.

This book represents an integration of personal and professional experiences that incorporates some of my earliest memories. I grew up in a family that, like many others, had its secrets. Family members used hushed voices about certain topics that others were not supposed to hear. As a boy I was interested in magic, magicians, and carnival games—the secrets of misdirection and illusion, as well as the unseen gimmicks and ruses that rigged the games of chance. As a young man I was drafted into the Army during the Vietnam War and assigned to duty near the DMZ in South Korea as a special agent in military intelligence. When I returned home I started a career in government service and completed a doctorate in public administration.

In my early career as an analyst and executive in the U.S. government, I had a chance to witness and learn at close hand the political behavior of public organizations. This led me to study organizational psychology and organization development. Later, as a professional consultant, I encountered covert processes while working with executives on organizational change in corporations around the world. All of these experiences, along with research about covert processes drawn from the social sciences, have informed the principles and practices presented here.

The Limits of Rationality

As a society we place great importance on being rational and logical. This is the primary reason that certain crucial elements may become covert during change initiatives. Presenting a rational argument is often done at the expense of attention to anything else—emotions, for instance. In many years of working with executives around the world, three aspects of organizational change have become increasingly clear to me:

1. Most change agents rely primarily on rational approaches to foster organizational change.

2. Most change initiatives actually involve significant non-rational dynamics and processes.

3. Most change agents still insist on operating as if organizational change is a purely rational process.

Time after time I have witnessed the over-emphasis on reason contribute to failed or ineffectual change initiatives. Because of their insistence on rational approaches, many change leaders are unable to see the non-rational dimensions of organizational change that are adversely impacting their initiatives.

Analyteks, Inc.

Analyteks, Inc., was a highly successful professional services company for over forty years. Analyteks' culture and management style were based on a small circle of entrepreneurial executives doing all the marketing and sales work. These executives would then provide instructions to highly educated analysts, who were expected to follow directions while applying their professional skills to assigned projects. This centralized model had for decades produced many notable accomplishments and steady growth.

Now, changes in the competitive landscape and new advances in technologies threatened Analyteks' success. After many quarters of decline, management announced the first cutbacks in the company's history. Anticipating the need for even more cutbacks, leadership decided that the analysts needed to become more entrepreneurial in their work so the company could continue to succeed in the new world they were facing.

Accordingly, the executives presented their case for more entrepreneurial behavior from the analysts at a series of company-wide meetings. Then they waited for behaviors to change. When nothing very different happened, they were confused. After all, they had clearly stated the reasons for change.

Some Often-Neglected Dimensions

What had the Analyteks executives failed to consider in their planning sessions? They had not thought about the differing self-interests of the executives and analysts and how those differences might impact support of the new directions. In fact, the analysts saw the call for them to be more entrepreneurial as a bailout for the failures of the executives.

One analyst summed it up with the comment: "When I joined Analyteks it was with the understanding that they would do the selling and I could work on neat projects." Furthermore, becoming sales people did not inspire the analysts, who wanted to do cutting-edge work and not just survive to sell "schlock services to make a buck."

Unfortunately, the analytical nature of the people and of the business culture, added to concerns about being seen as weak, prevented the analysts (and the executives, for that matter) from openly expressing their fears or their anger. Those feelings were covert, and thus there were no signals to alert the executives that they were on the wrong track. The top-down, centralized culture of Analyteks had helped to create mindsets in which analysts were not expected to be entrepreneurs. That was the job of the executives. In fact, it was considered unprofessional within the Analyteks culture for an analyst to "sell out by selling your work."

Finally, it would not be too great a stretch to speculate that unconscious processes involving denial or excessive rationalizations among the executives, who were facing failure for the first time in their careers, may have prevented a more carefully thought-out approach. Instead, the executives ended up repeating the very behavior they said they wanted to change. In the meetings they presented a rational plan, predicated on the assumption that they knew best, even as they called for more ideas and involvement from the analysts.

Beyond Good Reasons

The Analyteks case helps to illustrate the overt and covert dimensions of organizational change. Analyteks executives relied on their rational analysis of the situation to provide good *reasons* to persuade the analysts to change their behavior. Overlooked or hidden from consideration, however, were the *politics* of the situation, including the differing needs and interests of the analysts and executives. The absence of providing anything to really motivate or *inspire* the analysts to change their behavior, as well as the inability to express such *emotions* as fear, anger, or doubt, prevented important considerations from being overtly discussed.

The unaddressed organizational culture and *mindsets* about what constitutes prestigious and professional work made it virtually impossible for the analysts to "hear" the executives' reasoned analysis about the need to be more entrepreneurial. Finally, unconscious *psychodynamics* fueled by the stress and anxieties associated with the declining situation may have led to reduced or impaired abilities in the executive group and among the analysts to fully consider all aspects of the situation.

Dimensions of Change

Expressed in everyday language, the six dimensions that are always involved in organizational change are: reasons, politics, inspirations, emotions, mindsets, and psychodynamics. These are summarized in the accompanying table. As already noted, reason always gets the overt emphasis. The other five dimensions are frequently covert, despite their influence on achieving desired results. Let's look more closely at these dimensions to see how they impact organizational change.

Overt and Covert Dimensions of Organizational Change

Reasons	Politics	Inspirations	Emotions	Mindsets	Psychodynamics
Rational and analytic logics	Individual and group interests	Values-based and visionary aspirations	Affective and reactive feelings	Guiding beliefs and assumptions	Anxiety-based and unconscious defenses

Reasons

Most organizational change initiatives begin, and sometimes end untimely, with "making the case for change." This case for change is invariably a well-documented, logical analysis of the compelling reasons why the organization and the people in it must do something different. For example, the Analyteks executives might have said at some point:

> Due to the forces of globalization, information technology, and increased worldwide competitiveness, we must become more

entrepreneurial at all levels of the company. In order to do this we will, (a) pursue a new strategy, (b) adopt a new structure, (c) create a new reward and compensation system, (d) downsize, right-size, and contract out some functions. If we do these things well, then we will once again be successful and prosperous as an organization.

The unspoken part of this message, which can lead people to ignore important considerations, is: *We expect everyone to be logical and rational and accept the compelling reasons for what has to be done, and therefore not only understand and go along with the changes but even embrace them.* When this does not happen, as in the Analyteks case, change leaders are surprised. They may conclude that they are dealing with irrational resistance to change because their well-reasoned arguments are being ignored.

In response, some combination of three strategies is often pursued. First, change leaders emphasize the overwhelming logic and rationale for change with even more compelling analyses, educational efforts, and discussions. The thinking is something like: *If only we make the right case for change, people will understand what needs to be done and do it.*

Second, leadership may try addressing what they consider to be irrational resistance through venting or involvement sessions. Frequently these efforts receive less attention than the case for change itself, and they are quickly abandoned if they don't produce immediate results. Management thinks: *What's the use? Nothing will work. We are dealing with irrational resistance.*

Third, if reason and logic don't seem to carry the day, the change effort is aborted, abbreviated, or forced. *Well, people are just too emotional, so we need to. . . ."*

Although the rational case for change tends to be the most overt or visible dimension, covert elements also play a critical role in all organizational change initiatives. We will now discuss the five dimensions of covert behavior: internal politics, inspirations, emotions, mindsets, and unconscious defenses or psychodynamics. When these five dimensions are overlooked, they become traps that can block even the best-planned efforts.

Politics

Most organizations are managed based solely on rationality, defined roles, rules, expertise, and the good of the organization as a whole. Individuals and work units are discouraged from advancing their own interests. Actions based on your own interests are deemed to be "political," and being political is considered inappropriate behavior in most organizations. This set of beliefs also supports reliance on "making the case for change" through top-down initiatives.

In reality, people and work groups do consider their own needs and interests when they respond to organizational change initiatives. It is folly to assume otherwise. These needs and interests may sometimes be selfish or self-serving, but generally they simply reflect people of goodwill operating from a place rooted in their own experience. From their point of view, what others call resistance may be a well-intentioned attempt to keep the organization on the right track.

Who is to say that the change in question is not the selfish or self-serving initiative of an elite group of executives advancing their own interests over those of the organization as a whole? In the Analyteks case, one analyst was heard to comment: "When they came up with this new sales strategy, did they understand the impact it will have on the way we do our work as professional analysts, or were they just worried about their own bonuses?"

This orientation suggests a different model of organizations, one where it is assumed that people and groups act on their own needs and interests. In this model, political as well as rational processes are the ways through which organizations really operate.

The general distaste for recognizing and dealing with organizational politics is often evident in change efforts. In my experience, this is mostly associated with the mindset that organizations should be managed through reason and logic alone, and that politics is somehow "bad"—thus change planners often do not think in terms of political perspectives or organizational politics. *Others might stoop to do this, but we should not.* Consequently, when political processes of one kind or another emerge to challenge or disrupt a change effort, planners are unprepared to deal with what they experience as covert political dynamics.

Inspirations

Most change efforts include some kind of vision statement intended to capture the essence of the desired future state: *We will be the best (biggest, smartest, fastest, friendliest, most flexible, most knowledgeable) company in the world.* These statements are often a shorthand version of the case for change analysis: *Because of globalization, we need to be the best company in the world.* They are intended to help people think rationally about the change and become convinced to work toward it.

The difference between these kinds of vision statements and values-based and visionary aspirations is the difference between head and heart. Evoking values and aspirations is intentionally inspirational. Inspirational statements speak to our better selves, bypassing logic and striking a chord. When this occurs people feel compelled to make the desired change a reality. This happens because people are willing to work towards strongly held values or aspirations, sometimes despite rational logic. The analysts in Analyteks did not want to sell more "schlock services," but they might have strongly supported changes that would enable them to work toward providing customers with higher-quality products or services.

Enlisting positive values and aspirations is the province of the inspirational leader, not the analytical manager. Martin Luther King's "I Have a Dream" speech inspired people to change by evoking powerful shared values and aspirations, not by a rational analysis of prevailing conditions. Imagine the same speech if Dr. King had presented an analysis of the number or percentage of discriminatory events in the past year and the market forces that positively or negatively impacted a more just society! The power of inspiration to bring about change is that it does *not* appeal to reason and logic. Inspiration speaks to the aspects of people that want to do good things, want to be part of something bigger than themselves, and want to see their values, hopes, and dreams fulfilled.

Despite the power of inspiration, it is frequently ignored or muted in change efforts. When that happens, a potentially powerful force for change is underutilized or becomes an unexpressed covert dynamic. Even worse, change efforts sometimes fail because they unknowingly work *against* the strongly held, but unexpressed, values and aspirations of key employees or work groups.

The power of heart over head in organizational change is explained by John Kotter and Dan Cohen in their book *The Heart of Change* (2002). They assert that most change efforts are based solely on the core method of *analysis-think-change*, or what I have called "making the case for change," and that most change efforts fail as a result. In the *analysis-think-change* method people are given (1) a data-based, logical analysis of the situation and what needs to be different; it is then presumed that (2) the data and analysis will influence how people think; and then (3) this will lead to new thoughts that will produce changed behaviors and actions.

Contrasted with this is the core method of *see-feel-change*, which Kotter and Cohen claim is almost always associated with successful change efforts. In the *see-feel-change* method, people are (1) helped to see a compelling vision or situation needing to be addressed; then (2) that compelling vision or situation hits the emotions and evokes a gut-level response; and then (3) the emotionally charged response to the situation leads to changed behaviors and actions. They strongly advocate greater use of inspiration and emotion over reason and analysis in organizational change efforts. Engage the heart, not just the head!

Emotions

Similar to but different from visionary inspiration is the role of emotions in organizational change. To be more accurate, it is the *non*-role of emotions in organizational life. Historically, emotions have been viewed as the enemy of reason and thus to be overcome or suppressed. This attitude pervades the organizational world, where decision-making by logic and analysis—not emotion—is extolled as a virtue. Although emotions and feelings are an integral part of human life, they are generally considered to be anathema in the workplace, despite the recent importance placed on emotional intelligence. Consequently, whatever feelings and emotions exist related to a change effort, they tend to be hidden and expressed only in covert ways.

Many of the change leaders with whom I have been associated

have been less than eager to participate in open meetings because the sessions might become "too emotional." I recall a reluctant executive who, before an all-hands meeting, commented in an agitated voice: "If people are going to be emotional about these changes, then I don't want to deal with them. When they are ready to discuss things rationally and logically, I'll meet with them." Not surprisingly, three days later the all-hands meeting was indefinitely postponed "due to pressing business." An opportunity to engage the workforce in supporting the change had been missed for fear of overt emotionality.

Emphasizing reason and logic in organizational matters, while avoiding anyone who is too mad, glad, sad, or afraid, ensures that unexpressed emotions will go underground and covertly impact any change initiatives. Most organizational change consultants agree that people react to organizational change in ways similar to Elizabeth Kübler-Ross' (1973) stages of death and dying: denial, anger, bargaining, depression, acceptance, and, finally, adaptive behavior.

This analogy makes clear that many people will react initially with anger to the announcement of any significant organizational change and that this is normal and predictable. Thus it would be unreasonable to expect otherwise. Nonetheless, leaders often act as if they should be able to announce a change and then immediately enter into reasoned discussions with impacted employees about implementing the change. In this scenario, if the employees show any anger they are labeled as irrational, emotional, or resistant to change. A more savvy response would be that they are having normal human reactions that need to be acknowledged and addressed in some manner.

A comparison of two similar change situations illustrates the power of covert emotions in organizational change. I was working with two very different organizations, a not-for-profit service agency and a for-profit global corporation. Both organizations had concluded that, for better positioning in the marketplace, they needed to change their identity and their name. One had a name that limited who it could serve. The other had done market research and wanted to change its image from an old-line, slow, cold corporation into one that would be regarded as responsive, service-oriented, and warm.

In each case, months of research and analysis had been completed by internal task forces and outside expert reports. Furthermore, the respective executive teams and boards had agreed with the need to change the name and identity of the organization. In each case, the moment finally came for the executive team to make the proposed name change. In neither case was the name changed!

Instead, another round of discussion ensued, and again everyone expressed reasons for the change based on logic, need, and sound research. After this additional round of assurance that they were doing the right thing, once more the time came to take the vote. Again, in each case, the vote was delayed. The leaders of the meetings were perplexed, but to me they had appeared somewhat reluctant to take the vote.

At this point I wondered if there were unexpressed emotions about the impending loss of their long-established names and identities. In both cases I suggested that, having shared their *thoughts* about the name change, maybe they should also look at their *feelings* about the proposed change. After initial hesitation, people began to share how sad and depressed, and maybe even a little afraid, they were to do away with the old name. They went on to talk about how much they were attached to the old name and how things would not be the same using the new one.

These discussions went on for some time and allowed people to release a range of emotions that had previously been covert. Following a break, they came back and took the vote again. In both cases they voted to make the change. In both instances it is likely that unexpressed sadness, loss, and fear were covertly preventing the executives from acting on their reasoned analysis.

Mindsets

In addition to explicit reasoning, change initiatives are guided by unexamined or untested assumptions, beliefs, and premises. I will refer to them here as *mindsets*. Because people generally don't think about the underlying frameworks that guide the way they reason and interpret the world, mindsets have a profound (though often covert) impact on the ways we react to change possibilities.

In the form of *mental models,* they are "deeply ingrained assumptions, generalizations, or even pictures or images that influence how we understand the world and how we take action" (Senge, 1990, p. 8). In the form of *paradigms* or *worldviews,* they prevent people from imagining possibilities that exist outside of their unexamined assumptions. Expressed as organizational *cultures,* these covert beliefs, values, and assumptions guide and interpret the most fundamental aspects of organizational life. Individual and organizational mindsets can thus form covert conceptual traps that limit our thinking and require a mental revolution to change how we act and react in the world.

Chris Argyris was one of the first organizational researchers to point out the limiting power of hidden mindsets in organizations and advocated *double-loop learning* as a way to avoid such covert conceptual traps (1977). In essence, double-loop learning asks people to examine the assumptions they take for granted that may guide their current ways of thinking and to consider adopting new beliefs that would allow different possibilities to occur. Dramatic organizational change is only possible, says Argyris, when prevailing covert mindsets are made overt, challenged, and modified.

Without a change in mindsets, people will continue to see situations in the same way and develop the same responses no matter how much they may rationally or emotionally wish to change. I recall working in the early 1980s, shortly after the breakup of AT&T, with the executive team of one of the Baby Bells. Our task was to plan how to become a more customer-responsive organization.

The team worked hard, but moving toward "outside-in thinking" (*What do customers want and how can we provide it?*) from ingrained "inside-out thinking" (*What do we provide and how can we get customers to purchase it?*) proved to be an extremely difficult shift in mindset. All of their habitual ways of thinking about and addressing a situation were turned upside down. This became obvious when, in frustration, one of the executives turned to me and said: "Let's stop wasting our time trying to figure out what customers want. What we have to do is get them to buy more of what we have."

It is not unusual for planners and implementers of change to be limited in their thinking by covert mindsets that prevent truly transformational initiatives. It's not that such results are not wanted; it is simply that unexamined mindsets covertly prevent people from thinking outside the box. Stop and consider how many of the management initiatives and organizational forms that are currently accepted practice were virtually unthinkable twenty years ago. The shift from the capacity-driven, certainty-oriented, mass-production, industrial-age paradigm to the more customer-oriented, flexible, and customized paradigm of the current information age requires both a revolution in information technologies and a revolution in managerial mindsets. And, as more than one organization has discovered, installing new technologies can be much easier than changing prevailing mindsets.

Psychodynamics

No dimension is more covert, or less often addressed, than our unconscious reactions to change. This is related to the widespread taboo about dealing with—or even seriously speculating about—unconscious dynamics in a workplace setting. That's for employee assistance programs or personal counseling. A manager once asked me during a team-building session, when people seated in a circle were asked to share their perceptions of each other: "Is this going to become a shrink session?"

Addressing the overt and rational reasons for change is always a requirement for an organizational change effort. Considering the covert, unconscious reactions and dynamics is almost always considered off-limits in the workplace.

Despite this persistent taboo, there has been a great deal of research about the covert impacts of the unconscious on groups and organizations. Generally speaking, unconscious defenses against anxiety are a root aspect of psychodynamic phenomena at work. Because organizational change—from initially identifying new needs through implementing new ways of working—is likely to be anxiety producing, the possible impact of unconscious reactions must be considered. Of course some resistance may be consciously calculated, but some may be unconscious reactions to the anxieties triggered by organizational change, or even organizational life in general.

Taking a psychodynamic point of view, we should not be surprised if, during a meeting announcing a major change, an individual or even a whole group exhibits a variety of unconscious defense mechanisms. Maybe the group, instead of rationally working on how to implement the change, will engage in "fight or flight" behavior (by being argumentative or by avoiding the topic). Maybe an individual will engage in transference and begin to act as if the leader were a parent ("You always favor the marketing department"). Maybe a leader will repress feelings of anxiety about having to downsize fellow workers and compensate by acting overly logical and cool at a time when some warmth and emotions are needed ("Please report to human resources to finalize the paperwork").

Once, when I was in an internal staff position, I worked with a top executive who was leading a change effort. In meetings he constantly berated his direct reports, pointing out how incompetent they were, while posing as just the opposite. Privately, I inquired how he could ask his people to change when he presented himself as needing no changes. I suggested that perhaps, as an act of leadership, he needed to model how people could change themselves in order to produce organizational culture change.

In a moment of candor growing out of our long association, this leader revealed that he had to be "perfect" because his father had always berated him for not measuring up. This led to a discussion of "that was then and this was now." It also included a gentle inquiry to see if he had ever considered or sought counseling (the answer was yes) and how the present situation could be an unconscious trigger for past feelings and patterns of behavior.

The realization that he had to address some of his unresolved feelings and patterns from the past in order to be the leader he wanted to be in the present did not need any further prompting. He started the next meeting by talking about how everyone, including himself, needed to change their behaviors to implement the new culture.

A Checklist for Change

We have seen that one helpful way to begin thinking about organizational change is to insist on considering the influences of all six overt and covert dimensions. This means making sure that both rational and non-rational dimensions of change are fully considered. A simple checklist can remind everyone that organizational change is not likely to be successful without considering all six of the dimensions.

Six Dimensions of Organizational Change

1. Reasons: Rational and Analytic Logics

    Are we clear about our intended outcomes and criteria?

    Have we analyzed the forces and reasons for change related to our intended outcome and criteria?

    Have we considered all the options and selected the one most likely to succeed?

    Have we made a strong and persuasive case for change?

    Do we have a clear implementation plan and processes?

    Other:

2. Politics: Individual and Group Interests

    Who are the key stakeholders with interests related to this change and, based on their needs, how might they perceive this change?

    What sources of power or influence do they have to impact the change?

    How will we deal with each critical stakeholder to ensure support for the change?

    Will we need to modify our proposal to gain enough support by those who could block our plan?

    How will we continue to monitor the shifting needs, interests, and political processes as the change unfolds?

    Other:

3. Inspirations: Values-Based and Visionary Aspirations

    What are the key values and aspirations of organizational members?

    How will those values and aspirations be impacted or energized by the proposed change?

    How can we present or modify our proposed change to inspire and enlist people?

    Do we have leaders with the skills and abilities to inspire people about the change?

    How do we develop leaders with basic inspirational skills and abilities?

    Other:

(continues)

4.   Emotions: Affective and Reactive Feelings

Which people may become mad, glad, sad, or afraid due to the proposed change?

Do we understand and accept that emotional reactions are a normal reaction to change and loss?

How will we create settings where emotions can be expressed in constructive and appropriate ways?

Do we have leaders with the emotional intelligence and skills to deal with people who are emotional about change?

How do we develop leaders with basic emotional intelligence skills and abilities?

Other:

5.   Mindsets: Guiding Beliefs and Assumptions

What are the key assumptions and beliefs currently limiting the possibilities for change?

What are the alternative assumptions and beliefs underlying our change proposal?

How will we change people's mindsets to allow them to see the new possibilities?

Do we have leaders who are aware of their own mindsets and can practice double-loop learning as needed during the change effort?

How do we develop leaders with the ability to challenge their own thinking and strongly held assumptions and beliefs?

Other:

6.   Psychodynamics: Anxiety-Based and Unconscious Defenses

Do we understand and accept that there may be unconscious reactions by individuals and groups to our change proposal?

Do we know who might have the greatest anxieties, or be threatened the most, by our change proposal?

Do we understand enough of the basic manifestations of unconscious reactions to anxiety to recognize when logic and reason alone may not work?

Do we have leaders with enough emotional or psychological intelligence and skills to be able to deal at least on some level with the basic unconscious defenses they may encounter?

How do we develop leaders with enough basic emotional or psychological intelligence skills and abilities?

Other:

The purpose of such a checklist is to counterbalance the bias in most organizations toward expecting, or subtly demanding, only rational thinking and responses. It helps to remind us that non-rational, covert dimensions will be involved whether we like it or not. It also alerts us to anticipate the range of covert processes that may manifest themselves as we plan and manage organizational change.

Conclusion

Leaders, staff specialists, and consultants may be blindsided if they focus primarily on reason-based approaches to change. As we have seen, an array of hidden elements are likely at work whenever the need for change arises. Wisdom lies in anticipating and addressing the potential covert issues so that the following five dimensions do not derail a potentially positive change:

1. Individual and group interests that are actually or potentially impacted by the change (the **political** dimensions of change)

2. Values-based and visionary aspirations of members that may support or conflict with efforts (the **inspirational** dimensions of change)

3. Feelings of people about the change (the **emotional** dimensions of change)

4. Implicit beliefs and assumptions shaping how people think (the **mindsets** dimension of change)

5. Anxiety-based and unconscious defenses and reactions (the **psychodynamic** dimensions of change)

To be a successful agent of change, you must go beyond reason-based initiatives to address these five covert dimensions. Being blindsided by a surprise birthday party may be fun, but it is rarely fun when you are planning and implementing change.

CHAPTER 2

▶ # A Model for Understanding Covert Processes

This chapter introduces a multidimensional model that explains the sources and dynamics of all covert processes. Instead of addressing each of the five covert dimensions separately, the model reveals what they have in common. This model addresses three critical questions:

1. Why and how do things become covert?

2. What are the different types of covert processes?

3. How do different covert processes interact and manifest themselves?

This chapter provides a conceptual foundation for thinking about covert processes and how they may impact any change initiative.

The Covert Processes Model

A number of years ago, Judith Katz and I developed the Covert Processes Model to help us better understand, diagnose, and deal with the complex dynamics involved in all covert processes (Marshak and Katz, 2001). The model shows the fundamental sources and types of covert processes for individuals, groups, and organizations (see accompanying illustration). It is eclectic, drawing on a diverse set of psychological, sociological, and social-psychological theories to bring together in one framework a range of covert processes that are normally discussed separately. It is presented in everyday language and organized around a metaphor used almost everywhere to connote overt and covert dynamics in organizations.

The model uses the imagery of what's on-the-table or putting things on-the-table for overt processes. Consistent with that basic metaphor, things that are covert are located elsewhere (under-the-table, above-the-table). This allows the model to incorporate a complex understanding of covert dynamics while retaining the readily understood framework. We have found that the on-the-table and under-the-table imagery allows us to explore covert dynamics in workplace settings without having to use much psychological jargon.

The model assumes that covert processes can emerge from conscious, unconscious, and out-of-awareness dynamics. The multifaceted sources of covert processes led us to two critical realizations. First, no matter how hard you might try or how much you might wish, some things will always be covert in any social system. The second critical realization was that covert processes, despite prevailing sentiments to the contrary, are not inherently bad or evil.

Things may be hidden or out-of-awareness for a variety of reasons. In other words, covert processes simply "are," and involve anything that is not overt for whatever reasons. No negative value judgment is implied or assumed. Things may be hidden for good, bad, or unknown reasons. These two insights, as will be discussed later, have a fundamental impact on the way we think about and deal with covert dynamics during organizational change.

The Focal System and Field of Experience

The first step in understanding covert processes is to consider what the focal system is, and then consider its field of experience. *Focal system* is the term for the social unit on which you are focused. Are you focused on what's happening in the organization, in one of its work groups, in a specific individual, or in all three? As you use the model, you will sometimes find it necessary to shift your attention from one focal system to another.

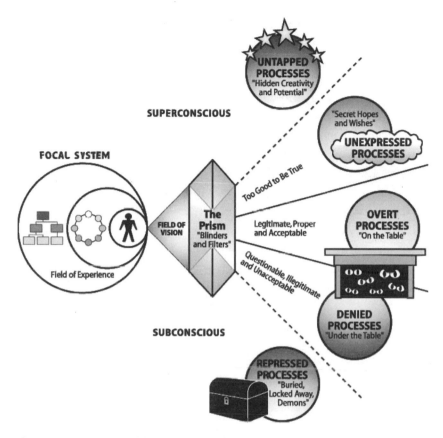

The Covert Processes Model. © 2001 Marshak & Katz.

The model is equally applicable whether you are working with an individual, a work group, or the organization as a whole. Sometimes your inquiry will be individually focused: *What's going on under-the-table with Jane?* Sometimes it will be work group focused; *What's going on under-the-table in Jane's sales team?* Finally, it could be organizationally focused: *What's going on under-the-table with respect to the sales function?*

The *field of experience* helps to define what is known and unknown to the focal system. Every individual, group, and organization is defined by its life and historical experiences. No individual, group, or organization will have been exposed to all there is to know, so there will always be hidden possibilities simply because they have not been part of the system's experience or knowledge base. For individuals, the field of experience is defined by such factors as age, education, religious training, race, gender, sexuality, socioeconomic status, professional identity, or family experiences. For groups and organizations, analogous factors might include age, type of business, demographics, and types of products or services provided.

The field of experience sets the limits that initially determine what is open (overt) or closed (covert) to consideration by the focal system. For example, a work group with a field of experience that includes a long history of autocratic bosses may find it difficult to work with any other leadership style. In such a case your attempts to introduce a different style may fall on deaf ears or be completely misunderstood. Likewise, an organization with a hundred-year history in a regulated industry might find the requirements of a deregulated and highly competitive market literally inconceivable—and hence "hidden" from consideration.

The Prism and Its Contents

What we actually perceive and how we make sense of the world is further filtered through a *prism* composed of individual, group, organizational, and societal lenses. The notion of the prism is drawn primarily from cognitive psychology, which asserts that all social experience is interpreted through internal belief structures. The contents of the focal system's prism thus become a primary determinant of how things will be seen and interpreted. Whether the glass is half full or half empty depends on your prism and not on the actual quantity of water in the glass. There are also a number of belief components that exist within the prism, as seen in the accompanying illustration. Each component plays a part in defining how things will be seen and interpreted by the focal system.

Childhood Lessons Learned

These include "tapes" and messages from parents, teachers, and other authority figures about what is right and wrong and how you should behave. For example, we were all told when we were young how to be a good little boy or a good little girl: *Always play nice. Don't get dirty. Take care of your brother. Do what you're told. Don't get into fights.* In

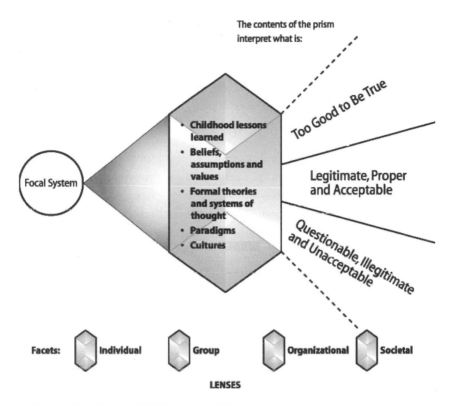

The contents of the prism interpret what is:

Too Good to Be True

Legitimate, Proper and Acceptable

Questionable, Illegitimate and Unacceptable

Focal System

- **Childhood lessons learned**
- **Beliefs, assumptions and values**
- **Formal theories and systems of thought**
- **Paradigms**
- **Cultures**

Facets: Individual Group Organizational Societal

LENSES

Contents of the Prism. © 2001 Marshak & Katz.

addition, we were taught ways to navigate successfully in the world: *If I take care of others, people will be nice to me.* Often these early lessons remain unexamined in our prisms, but they still influence our adult behavior. Consider how we learned to look first left and then right when crossing the street, and how difficult it is to break the habit when we visit other countries where they drive on the opposite side of the road!

Beliefs, Assumptions, and Values

Beliefs, assumptions, and values comprise the broadest array of concepts that order, judge, link, and explain events. This array also encompasses such things as biases, prejudices, and habitual thought patterns. And, while some beliefs, assumptions, and values were carried forward from childhood, some are of recent origin. All have the impact of both organizing and limiting your experience and responses. Consider the power of the values learned by the Depression-era generation about thriftiness and how that shaped the way they engaged the world. For many of that generation, debt and credit cards were never an option.

Formal Theories and Systems of Thought

These include all aspects of what you have learned through formal education, as well as exposure to religious, philosophical, and professional ideals and concepts. Theories and systems of thought help shape the way you look at the world and your beliefs about how things are related to each other. What someone learns in business school about the duty to provide shareholder value, for example, can have a profound impact on later managerial choices about meeting the needs and interests of employees (Ghoshal, 2005).

Paradigms

Paradigms are out-of-awareness conceptual models that guide the way you organize and think about some classes of phenomena. Formal theories and systems of thought develop within the framework of a particular paradigm. It is virtually impossible to "see" something that does not exist within your operating paradigm. A change in paradigm can be so powerful that it is usually considered revolutionary or transformational in impact. Currently many organizations are shifting from industrial-age paradigms about management and organization to newer paradigms involving virtual organizations, telecommuting, and off-shoring, for example.

Organization and Societal Cultures

Culture includes taken-for-granted assumptions about the most basic aspects of life in the organization and society: *Are people inherently good or evil? Is competition or cooperation best? Is directive or participatory leadership better? How do we define success in this organization? What is taboo around here?*

Until you encounter another culture, these aspects of your prism generally go unquestioned. The familiar change theory of unfreeze-movement-refreeze, for example, assumes change happens through an episodic, linear process, whereas in some traditional cultures change is assumed to be both continuous and cyclical.

Impacts of the Prism

It is primarily through our prisms that a number of covert processes begin to take shape. Anything your prism defines as legitimate, proper, acceptable, and reasonable will become overt and can be placed on-the-table for open discussion and engagement. Anything your prism defines as either unacceptable or too good to be true will be un-discussable, will then become covert, and will be kept off-the-table. If a group's prism defines something as unacceptable, then even if someone puts it on-the-table it will be quickly knocked off or ignored.

R.J: *Hey, we didn't discuss the criteria for bonuses.*

H.D: *Now that we have finished with bonuses, let's move on to another topic.*

In short, the contents of our prisms help us to interpret and deal with the world, but they also serve as blinders and filters covertly preventing us from considering or discussing certain possibilities.

If the unexpressed beliefs in a work group's prism prohibit open discussion of emotions as *unacceptable,* then most feelings will need to be disguised, denied, or expressed covertly, perhaps through passive-aggressive behavior. Likewise, an organization's culture may imply that win-win collaborative relationships between the union and management is pie-in-the-sky and therefore too good to be true. If so, then in that organization contrary beliefs or courses of action will become covert or go unconsidered.

Overt Processes: What Goes On-the-Table

What will be overt, or on-the-table, therefore, includes anything that the individual, group, or organization prism(s) defines as *acceptable, proper, reasonable and legitimate.* The range of what's permitted on-the-table will vary from individual to individual, group to group, and organization to organization, depending on what is valued in that focal system and on the tacit agreements among the members of the system.

In a work group where examining the team's strengths *and* weaknesses is considered appropriate behavior, you would expect a team review meeting to include open discussions of areas of success and areas to improve. This would be different from a work group where discussing strengths is considered to be somehow inappropriate or unacceptable, perhaps because it is "not needed." If the work group's prism questioned the value of acknowledging strengths, people would think to themselves: *Why talk about what people are doing well? Focus on what needs to be improved.* Any attempts to discuss strengths might then be knocked off the table in favor of discussing individual and team weaknesses. Likewise, in many organizations, discussions related to the bottom line are always overtly on-the-table, but discussions about values are sometimes considered to be too "airy-fairy" to be discussed for very long, if at all.

Covert Processes: What Stays Off-the-Table

Topics, thoughts and behaviors that cannot be put on-the-table for open discussion become hidden. They do not, however, go away. Instead they continue to exist and are often expressed covertly. The five principal manifestations, or places to look for, covert processes are: (1) things that are out-of-awareness and located in the prism, such as mindsets; (2) things that are denied and located under-the-table, such as negative emotions or politics; (3) things that are unexpressed and above-the-clouds, such as inspirations; (4) things that are repressed and buried in the subconscious, such as deep fears and anxieties; and (5) things that are untapped and in the superconscious, such as "the farthest reaches of human nature" or our "higher selves."

Out-of-Awareness, In the Prism

Significantly, the existence of the prism and its powerful influences is itself covert to most people. People don't usually think about the implicit mindsets that guide their day-to-day thoughts. When the contents of the prism are left unexamined, however, the focal system's behavior will be controlled, and limited, by unseen and untested constraints. Despite the power of the prism, people are often unaware of its pervasive impacts.

Meanwhile, outsiders with different prisms may be confused as to why relatively obvious possibilities are systematically ignored. The members of the focal system may not be able to get their thinking out-of-the-box, but an outsider may see that everyone is struggling to push open a locked door while ignoring an open window. Finally, the ways in which a focal system's prism is guiding and limiting how it thinks about and deals with organizational change is usually completely out of awareness unless someone questions the tacit assumptions.

Things Denied and Under-the-Table

Hidden under-the-table are those topics, thoughts, and behaviors considered too risky to address openly. These become covert because of the fear of punishment for openly engaging in something believed to be inappropriate or unacceptable. People in a work group, for example, may refer to difficulties with another department but feel it is inappropriate to talk about them openly in a negative way. Likewise, an obvious flaw in a plan may not be raised if the prism of the powerful boss includes a belief that challenging feedback from subordinates is unacceptable. Consider also an organization whose prism includes the belief that leaders worthy of their positions are supposed to have all the answers. In such organizations, elaborate covert processes will evolve to keep spontaneous issues off-the-table and protect senior managers from appearing stupid or incapable. There will be "no surprises" and things will be worked out before meetings.

When all members of a focal system have an interest in keeping something hidden for fear of the consequences, there is likely to be covert collusion. Covert collusion is especially common in settings where there is a high degree of suspicion. Members of a work group who withhold needed information or maneuver to ensure that certain topics are not fully addressed in a meeting are two examples of this type of covert process.

Another manifestation of denied processes occurs when the focal system, or some of its members, believe their purposes can best be achieved when not everyone knows what is going on. This often occurs in focal systems where there are competitive dynamics related to power, rewards, and resources. In such settings, individuals may act secretly to advance their own agenda. Individuals or groups acting in this way are considered to be "out for themselves" or engaged in "politics." Although this is only one type of covert dynamic, it usually comes to mind first when people think about covert processes.

Unexpressed and Above-the-Clouds

A third, often-overlooked, covert process involves the focal system's *secret hopes and wishes* that are hidden above-the-clouds. The prisms of individuals, groups, or organizations often contain tacit beliefs that it is inappropriate to express positive or optimistic thoughts. Consequently, desires to reach new heights, to express pride in accomplishments, or to express altruistic values or hopes for great achievements will be kept off the table. A focal system's most optimistic hopes and wishes—and anything considered to be too good to be true—will be kept covert out of fear of ridicule. People who enthusiastically express positive thoughts and ideas risk being labeled naive, unrealistic, or a stargazer.

In many work teams and organizations, attempts to create and express inspirational visions routinely fail because they are considered to be "too far out" or "not grounded in reality." Altruistic values may be ridiculed for having little or nothing to do with the bottom line. The unexpressed "too good to be true" aspect of covert processes is a reminder that not everything covert is bad. People hide their valuables as well as their vulnerabilities and vices.

Repressed and Buried in the Subconscious

At a deeper level, hiding in our unconscious, are things that are unacceptable to acknowledge. Psychoanalysts, beginning with Freud, described the unconscious as including powerful needs and drives that are so unacceptable they have been repressed, buried, and locked away, but still have a strong hold on our day-to-day behavior. Focal system defense mechanisms such as projections and compensatory behaviors are common manifestations of this type of covert process.

Groups that claim everything is fine while they drive themselves relentlessly, with no acknowledgment of the emotional, psychological, or physical toll, are likely to be under the influence of unconscious covert processes. For example, work teams operating in dangerous situations may take unnecessary risks as a show of bravado to compensate for their very real, but repressed, fears.

Individuals and groups may also project onto others their own unacceptable-to-acknowledge attributes. For example, the undesirable characteristics attributed to another work group (*They are selfish, ruthless, and only out for themselves*) may be nothing more than an unconscious defense mechanism wherein an unacceptable aspect of your own work group is projected onto someone else. In reality it may be your work group, not the other, that has needs for power and competitive victory at all costs.

Things Untapped in the Superconscious

This aspect of the Covert Process Model is based on the idea of a positive unconscious in which a focal system is in denial about, or repressing, its *positive* attributes. It is described in psychosynthesis, a spiritual psychology developed by Roberto Assagioli, who was a contemporary of Freud and Jung. To distinguish the positive aspects of the unconscious from the more negative aspects associated with the subconscious, it is called the superconscious. Both represent unconscious or psychodynamic phenomena. The superconscious contains creativity, talent, and as-yet-undiscovered dimensions that could help the focal system realize its full potential or its spiritual and higher purposes. Hidden away and not fully tapped are the outer limits of the focal system's creativity, synergy, and abilities.

The untapped possibilities, even though involving positive attributes, stay covert because it is simply unbelievable or unacceptable to imagine that such things could be true. For example, the possibilities of creating collaborative, synergistic alliances between producers and suppliers, supported by just-in-time inventory systems, were unimaginable not very many years ago. Similarly the possibility that a work team could have the competencies to be both innovative and self-managed is a relatively recent awareness for many teams and organizations.

All of these covert processes have several things in common. They are generally hidden from public discussion. They limit choices, block creativity, and can trap the focal system in repetitive and self-defeating behavior. They are not easily identified unless you know where to look. They are ubiquitous, always impacting what is said and done.

The Model in Action: A Case Illustration

The Covert Processes Model integrates a wide range of behavioral science theories to explain the dynamics of covert processes in individuals, groups, and organizations. It can help you to see how and why covert processes exist in all social systems, and where to look for them. Although the model is a static representation of different elements organized around the "on-the-table" metaphor, in use it invites dynamic consideration of covert processes at work. The case of the Whiz Tech Corporation illustrates this.

Whiz Tech Corporation

The Whiz Tech Corporation (WTC) is a high-tech company providing information technology services to a range of customers. Its growth had recently stagnated as competition increased from start-ups with more innovative solutions, glitches in the delivery of services began to erode customer confidence, and talented employees looking for cutting-edge projects began to leave the company. To address the situation, top executives held a series of meetings. They launched several initiatives, including a cross-sectional task force to study whether WTC needed a new vision for the future. After much study and analysis, the task force concluded that a new vision was desirable and went on a three-day retreat to develop it.

The retreat setting provided a fresh outlook and a welcome break from the office. Following a number of exercises designed to loosen their thinking, the task force forged a new vision statement. The statement was far more inspirational than anything WTC was used to; it spelled out values associated with technological prowess and with delivering innovative solutions that would made both customers and employees happy.

With great enthusiasm the task force presented their new vision to top management. The executive team appeared receptive to the new vision but they expressed a few concerns. Several executives wondered about the ab-

---

sence of references to profitability and "efficiency-type criteria," while others wondered whether WTC could deliver on the new vision. These comments were not discussed, however, and they decided to go forward with the new vision.

Proposed New Vision

The Whiz Tech Corporation provides cutting-edge solutions that continually amaze our global customers. Our solutions draw on:

- Our unparalleled technological prowess,
- Our ability to innovate and be creative,
- Our commitment to rapid and reliable performance, and
- A workplace that encourages fun, outstanding performance, and motivated, happy employees.

The leaders developed an implementation plan to have middle managers present the new vision to their work groups over the following three months. But implementation did not go as planned because several managers indicated they were too busy delivering results to their customers to hold a meeting on the "vision thing." Employees generally liked the energy of the new vision, but they openly wondered if anything would be different and, conversely, worried about changes coming too quickly.

Eventually, the new vision was presented to all employees. Everyone then returned to what they had been doing and nothing much happened with the new vision after that. There was no follow-up to bring WTC's culture, policies, structure, and ways of working into alignment with the new vision's aspirations and ideals.

The new vision statement hung on the walls of the conference rooms but it was not incorporated into the way WTC did its work. Competitors continued to make inroads, bureaucracy and a lack of innovation still created problems with customers, and talented people left in even greater numbers. After a while the top executives of Whiz Tech met once again to discuss how they could change the organization to be more innovative, to be more competitive, and to attract and retain top talent.

Applying The Covert Processes Model

Let's look at the Whiz Tech situation through the Covert Processes Model. The primary focal systems are the WTC executive team and the total organization. First, we note the rational discussions that led to the decision to commission a task force to reexamine the corporate vision. In the prism of Whiz Tech executives, delegating the development of a new corporate vision to a cross-sectional task force was a legitimate thing to do. Having a task force meet in a retreat setting was also clearly acceptable. At the retreat, the operating prism of the task force became somewhat different from the normal WTC prism. The various exercises and norm-setting activities they engaged in together led the task force to adopt working beliefs and assumptions that included: *It's OK to have fun; Tapping into employees' pride is more important than anything else; Have no limits, anything is possible; We are saving the company; People will really get behind what we are doing because this is what they really want.* Thus the new setting and activities helped create a different operational prism to guide their work as a task force. This allowed new ideas to be put on-the-table, engaged, and ultimately embraced.

When the vision was brought back to the sponsoring executives, however, the normal Whiz Tech prism took over to guide what would happen next. Thus the prism of the executives reviewing the task force's effort had different contents that were less accepting of the new vision. The executives' collective prism included such beliefs and assumptions as: *Work is serious business and fun is frivolous; We are charged with making money for our shareholders, not making people happy; Inspirational visions are silly, it's hard numbers and goals that matter; If we implement this vision, I am not sure I will know how to manage in the new ways it calls for; This whole task force thing was Pat's idea, not mine; Never publicly criticize a fellow executive; If we commission something we are expected to endorse and support it; If I raise any questions about the vision I will be attacked for not supporting the team.*

From the perspective of a top team with these assumptions and beliefs, the proposed vision raised a number of serious doubts and concerns. However, their prism also included beliefs that prevented open discussion of their doubts, so many concerns were un-discussable and thus had to remain covert.

Some of the doubts that were openly raised by the executives in the meeting had to do with the vision being too good to be true: *Isn't it too "airy-fairy" for a high-tech company of information technology geeks? Can we really run a company on values and inspirations? Could this really be the answer to our corporate problems?*

Other doubts that were not openly discussed had to do with questionable or unacceptable thoughts and feelings. These were concealed or denied in the meeting, but expressed privately and confidentially: *This was Pat's idea and I don't like Pat. I'm afraid I wouldn't be able to fit in if the new vision became a reality. Did we really let these crazy people go off in the woods and come back with something as soft and squishy as this to be the answer to our problems? I'm angry at what we got back but afraid to speak up.*

Because the operating prism of the top team could not allow open expression of these kinds of comments, they were not put on-the-table and fully engaged: *Never publicly criticize a fellow executive. If we commission something we are expected to endorse and support it. If I raise a question about the vision I will be attacked for not supporting the team.* Instead of working through the issues, the executives' concerns and feelings became covert and were expressed indirectly. As time went by there was less-than-enthusiastic support from some of the executives for the new vision, a few became very busy with other things, and still others tacitly waited for the whole thing to die for lack of commitment and resources.

When implementation of the vision moved to middle managers and their work groups, similar doubts and concerns emerged through the prisms of the people impacted. In addition, the middle managers—as many of them privately complained—did not have the skills to handle the challenges and emotions coming from their employees. The managers kept this under-the-table in fear they would be seen as not measuring up. The middle managers also picked up on the subtle and not-so-subtle signals that top management was not fully committed to the new vision. Many of them interpreted the vision as another "flavor of the month," believing it was still most important to follow the rules and make your numbers. Thus, downplaying or avoiding the implementation meetings was a sensible, although covert, strategy to deal with the mixed messages they were receiving.

Learning from the Whiz Tech Case

A quick lesson from the Whiz Tech case is that simply developing, and trying to implement, a new vision will not lead to change if the prisms of key people or the entire organization don't support the new ideas. The new vision may get special attention initially, but ultimately the change effort will be knocked off-the-table because prevailing mindsets simply do not allow it. Note that the absence of real commitment may never get openly expressed if beliefs and norms exist that don't permit it. Instead the reactions and responses will stay off the table, become covert, and leave the change advocates wondering what is going on.

You cannot take something that is "too good to be true" from above-the-clouds, put it on-the-table, and expect it to stay there without further support. You need to account for any under-the-table concerns that may be seen as too risky to discuss. You may also need to examine the focal system's prism to see if there are any beliefs and assumptions that need to be challenged or modified in some way. Chapters 7 and 8 discuss how to do this.

Conclusion

No matter how much a focal system seeks to change (that is, the overt message, on-the-table, is the desire to change) often covert processes work to maintain the status quo. Because *all* significant change involves covert processes, it is critical to consider what is overt and covert on all levels. What is in the prism, what is on-the-table, what is under-the-table, what is repressed and buried, and what lies in the unexpressed or untapped hopes, dreams, and potential of individuals, groups, and the organization? The more you develop your understanding of the nature of covert processes, recognizing how they operate, and develop skills to better address them, the more effective you will be in leading organizational change efforts.

CHAPTER 3

▶ # Cues and Clues

How do you go about detecting the presence of a covert dynamic at work in an individual, group, or organization? After all, when something is covert it is hidden or out-of-awareness. This chapter introduces a way of thinking that will help you to generate hunches about when a covert dynamic is at work, even when it is not clearly visible or announced in some way.

Diagnosing Covert Processes

The orientation required to develop hunches about possible covert dynamics runs somewhat counter to the way we typically look at things. What do we usually do? We look for observable indicators that something is going on and then come to some conclusion about what those indicators may mean. We look for what stands out in all the information in ways that suggest something important may be happening. We observe that sales have gone up or down, that people have come late or early to a client meeting, that a new structure is or is not working well.

In the language of Gestalt psychology, we pay attention to what is *figure* more than what is *ground*. What stands out from the background draws our attention. To develop hunches about covert dynamics, we need to reverse this tendency. Instead of focusing on what stands out, we need to notice the background, or what is missing. Instead of seeing the leaves on the tree, we need to be able to see the spaces between the leaves.

Another insight from Gestalt psychology about human perception helps explain why this can be difficult. People fill in empty spaces automatically. We all have a natural inclination to form *gestalts,* or "wholes," to fill in gaps, to complete things. The human eye literally has a blind spot in the retina where the optic nerve is located. We don't notice this gap in our vision because our brains automatically fill in the empty space. Similar tendencies occur when people almost automatically fill in empty spaces in data and conversations. You might not notice that something important was left out of a conversation: *Yes, now that you point it out, I know they didn't actually say it, but that's what they must have meant.* You might not notice that someone was ignored: *Oh, I thought we heard from everyone when we went around the table.* You might fill in on your own some missing information in a report: *I just assumed they meant to include that information.*

Developing hunches about the existence of covert processes requires overriding this natural tendency. You see a hidden dynamic or covert process by noticing what is missing. Once you see that something is missing, you can speculate about why it is missing and what you might do about it. Furthermore, as will be explained shortly, you notice something is missing because "normally" it should be there.

Diagnostic Formula

The orientation needed to see what is not there can be expressed as a formula for detecting covert processes. This formula serves as a tool to remind us of the ways of thinking needed to see, hear, or feel what is missing and possibly covert (Marshak and Katz, 1997). Expressed simply, the formula is this: The *cues and clues* that something is missing is a *function* of considering the expected *patterns* of behavior given the specific *context* of a situation, and then noting any *emphases* or *omissions* in those patterns. The accompanying table summarizes this formula. Let's look at all aspects of the formula and explore how they work together to generate hunches.

The Covert Processes Diagnostic Formula

Covert Process Clue = F [(P)(C) · (E/O)]			
Patterns	**Context**	**Emphases**	**Omissions**
Sequence, relationships, configuration, repetition, theories, shapes, symbols, etc.	Purpose, players, pecking order, place, phase, procedures, past, part of system, possibilities, etc.	What is played up, pursued, in-depth, proclaimed, loud, pointed out, prominent, etc.	What is played down, avoided, glossed over, denied, soft, ignored, in the background, etc.

Patterns

Noticing patterns involves paying attention to recurring sequences, relationships, configurations, or other regularities related to topics, behaviors, or issues. For example, a pattern observed in many groups who are avoiding conflict is that whenever a discussion begins to get heated and angry someone cracks a joke. Patterns may be observed in or between individuals, groups, and the organization.

- **Individual patterns.** Recurring patterns of behavior by an individual may signal individual covert processes. For example, we notice that Pat behaves in an aggressive or passive-aggressive fashion toward anyone in a position of authority, anytime, anywhere. This suggests that Pat has some covert issues with authority.

- **Interpersonal patterns.** Recurring patterns of behavior between the same individuals, which do not occur when they interact with others, may signal interpersonal covert processes. For example, we observe that Lee and Chris constantly question and challenge each other and that this does not occur between Lee or Chris and anyone else. This may signal that there are hidden or unspoken issues between these two people.

- **Group patterns.** Recurring patterns of behavior exhibited by different individuals in the same work group usually indicate group covert processes. For example, you notice that every time someone on your task force initiates an idea someone else questions whether it will work. The person doing the challenging may differ each time, but the pattern of initiating and being challenged remains constant. This suggests some type of covert group process related to such issues as power, authority, or inclusion.

- **Organizational patterns.** Recurring patterns of behavior exhibited by different individuals, in different work groups, at different levels, throughout an organization, often suggest organizational covert processes. For example, as you move about the organization you notice that everyone, everywhere, talks and behaves in a way that indicates top leadership is supposed to have all the answers. People defer or refer all types of problems, both large and small, "upstairs."

Paying attention to patterns also means being aware of relevant formal theories and models that describe how things should occur "normally." Formal theories and models describe how something is expected to happen based on many observations of the same phenomena. One example is Tuckman's (1965) theory about the pattern of small group development, wherein groups move through the stages of forming, storming, norming, and performing. If this pattern is not followed, something covert could be going on that is altering or influencing the "normal" process of team development. The same would be true of theories about individual and organizational behavior. They all imply a rough template or pattern of what should be "normal" and expected. When the pattern of what is expected does not unfold, it is a clue that a hidden dynamic may be at work.

Context

Paying attention to context involves interpreting patterns in terms of the milieu that "frames" the situation (Goffman, 1974). The meaning of a particular pattern of behavior could be different depending upon the time, place, setting, people, roles, relationships, or part of the system involved. For example, referring things upstairs in a crisis situation might be interpreted differently than during routine times. The context gives meaning to the behavior, but—and this is an important point to understand—it is the context *from the frame of reference of the focal system* that matters.

How might the focal system be framing or experiencing the situation? Does it see opportunities, or threats? An outside observer may have a set of expectations about the various roles and responsibilities on a task force that could be different from the task force members themselves. The outside observer may then misunderstand the meaning of something to the focal system because it is interpreted out of context. Put simply, behaviors in one context may have different meanings in a different context.

To the extent possible, then, you need to be able to enter into the frame of reference of the focal system to look for covert processes successfully. Knowing that your team is meeting at a time when the organization is facing significant downsizing is an important contextual factor for understanding what is or is not happening. Likewise, knowing such contextual factors as that the team is the finance committee, or it's the first team meeting, or it's an emergency team meeting, all need to be factored into the diagnostic equation.

Emphases and Omissions

Finally, paying attention to emphases and omissions involves noting what is overly emphasized or noticeably downplayed or absent in an expected pattern. When the focal system seems to overemphasize one thing, it may mean that something else is being hidden or compensated for. Recall the line from Hamlet: "Methinks the lady doth protest too much."

Another example arises when members of a work group stress their competencies and past successes, perhaps because they secretly fear they may be unable to handle a new problem. Their self-doubts and fear of failure are being covered up by special proclamations of their skills and abilities. Likewise, emphatic denials, such as the Shakespeare "protest too much," are worth noting.

Omissions can be potent signals. Something that would be "normal" in a particular context is absent ("The dog didn't bark"). A section of the report is missing. An executive who shows up for every meeting is absent without notification. We may not know the reasons, but such omissions point toward something covert. Having noted a seemingly significant omission, we can speculate about what covert processes may be present, and why, and what to do about it.

A situation where people don't discuss team leadership when the team is floundering, though they have discussed it at other times, is an omission worth noting. Are there unspoken fears about questioning leaders, or about raising needs for power and control? Is there an unspoken issue about trusting the team's leader? Are there cultural prohibitions about directly challenging leaders? If there is a possible solution that "normally" would be raised but isn't (*Let's train them to do it better),* might there be a hidden assumption (*You can't teach an old dog new tricks)?* It could also imply politics (*Don't give the initiative to human resources)* or repressed self-doubts (*Could I learn how to do it better?).* Additional data will be needed to develop good hunches about the specific reasons something is covert. The first and most important step, however, is to see what is missing.

Diagnosis in Action

In using the Covert Processes Diagnostic Formula

$$\text{Clue(s)} = F[(P)(C) \bullet (E/O)]$$

the potential existence of a covert process is revealed by observing any overemphasis or omission in an expected pattern, given the specific context. This method of diagnosis is hardly an exact science, but it is an art you can practice and learn. In applying the formula, you will benefit from a broad knowledge of contexts and patterns. Thus, the wider your experience and theory base about individual, group, and organizational behavior, the greater your ability to recognize what is expected and thus what might be overemphasized or omitted. Most readers will quickly recognize the emphases and omissions in the following two examples because they are familiar with both the pattern and context:

- 1, 2, _, 4, 5, _,7, 8, _,10 (Based on the expected numeric sequence, the numbers 3, 6, and 9 are missing.)

- Forming, Norming, Norming!, Performing (Based on Tuckman's theory, storming is missing and norming is strongly emphasized.)

However, many readers might miss or misinterpret the hidden element denoted by the question mark (?) in the following example, unless they knew the context or recognized the pattern:

- X, +, 10 = ?

One possible answer is that it is an algebraic equation of some sort adding an unknown, X, to the number 10 resulting in the quantity (X + 10). This looks familiar, except for the commas after the X and the plus sign. If, however, the reader knew the context (say a cross-cultural training course), and also Roman (X), Chinese (+), and Arabic (10) numerals, the pattern, and therefore the missing element becomes clear. Each symbol is a different way of writing the quantity *ten* (X, +, 10 = Ten). Thus, knowledge of context and recognition of a pattern(s) is a prerequisite for both noting and interpreting the potential meaning of an emphasis or omission.

Another type of example comes from a group that, as a warm-up exercise, listed all the subgroups that made up their total group. A list of over twenty items was produced, including men and women, locals and out-of-towners, smokers and nonsmokers, and late-niters and early-risers. Not included on this fairly comprehensive list was any mention of the visible racial and ethnic differences among members of the group.

When this omission was pointed out, one white woman quickly and emphatically asserted, "That's because we don't see them as different from us." This was met with an even more emphatic response from an African American woman, who countered, "How can you negate me by not seeing who I really am?" Given the context of visible demographic differences and the exhaustive pattern of the list, the omission of racial/ethnic subgroups was a clue that there might be some covert processes related to racial issues in the group. Sometimes what's missing says a whole lot more than what's present.

The following case offers an opportunity to practice diagnostic thinking about covert processes. First a situation is presented, and then more information about the context, patterns, and emphases/omissions is added, to demonstrate how they help to develop hunches. Here again are the five types and locations of covert processes to help you speculate about what might be going on as the information unfolds:

1. Things that are out-of-awareness and located in the prism

2. Things that are denied and located under-the-table

3. Things that are unexpressed and located above-the-clouds

4. Things that are repressed and located in the subconscious

5. Things that are untapped and located in the superconscious

---

Alpha Corporation

The Situation

Six members of a team are meeting to discuss an organizational problem. One member of the team is missing. People are rationally addressing a problem but quickly get sidetracked. There are frequent references to past successes by the team and little sense of urgency in the meeting. After about an hour the meeting ends with no decisions, other than to make sure the missing member is informed about what was discussed.

Before reading further, what are some of your initial or intuitive hunches about what may be going on in this situation? What do you think may be some specific covert processes at work in this situation: things that might be out-of-awareness, denied, unexpressed, repressed, or untapped? Notice how difficult it is to assess what may be going on without more information. What additional information about the context(s) would help you develop better hunches?

Some Contextual Factors

This is the seven-member executive team of Alpha Corporation. The corporation is facing a difficult financial situation and the committee has convened for the third time to address the issue. A change in the corporation's no-layoff policy is needed and morale is at an all-time low. The question is no longer whether to downsize, but how deeply to cut. The history and culture of Alpha emphasize paternalistic, top-down leadership with decisions carried out quickly and efficiently. Executives are selected for their rational problem-solving skills and ability to get things done. The missing member of the team is the CEO.

What are your thoughts now about what may be going on covertly in the Alpha Corporation executive team? What other contextual information do you wish you had? Now that you have this much information, what are your hunches about specific covert processes that may be at work? What patterns would be helpful to know more about if you want to develop better hunches?

Some Patterns

This team has a range of historic patterns that might be relevant. Typically, there are one-hour and three-hour executive committee meetings. The one-hour meetings are "business-as-usual" meetings; three-hour meetings usually involve major decisions or strategic choices. Executive committee meetings almost always result in decisions being made and responsibilities being assigned. During discussions, people frequently talk about the future in problem-solving ways. The members of the executive committee are task-oriented and meetings have a no-nonsense, let's-get-on-with-it tone. Finally, no one has ever missed an executive team meeting in the past three years.

Given these historic patterns, what strikes you as different about this situation? How are your initial thoughts being refined and shaped by this additional information? What further information, about what kinds of patterns, do you wish you had?

Some Emphases and Omissions

Given the context and past patterns, several things stand out either through emphasis or omission. Things **emphasized** include:
- It was a one-hour meeting, implying business-as-usual.
- The team tried to work rationality, but got sidetracked.
- Team members talked mostly about past successes.
- The pace of the meeting suggested little urgency.
- The only decision made was to inform the missing member.

(continues)

(continued)

Things **omitted** include:

- It was not scheduled as a three-hour (major decision) meeting though the company was in crisis.

- Despite the traumatic circumstances, no one expressed emotion (anger, fear, sadness) about the impending layoffs.

- There was no discussion of the future or concerns about their competence to address the future.

- The team made no decisions about what to do and gave no assignments.

- No one discussed why the CEO was missing for the first time.

What hunches are you now considering about possible covert dynamics at work in this situation? What additional data or observations do you wish you had, and how might you get them? Note especially how paying attention to the combined effects of context, patterns, and emphases and omissions helps in developing more focused hunches.

Some Hunches

Clearly, a wide range of hunches could be developed based on the limited data given to you about the Alpha Corporation. The following are some hunches to add to your own about possible covert dynamics that could be at work in the Alpha executive team given the situation, context, patterns, and emphases/omissions.

1. Alpha has a top-down culture, so team members might implicitly assume nothing can be done without the missing CEO and therefore they are going through the motions in the meeting *(out-of-awareness assumption in their prism)*.

2. Under the circumstances, most people would have some emotional reactions to the crisis. If these reactions are present, however, they are not being voiced. Consequently, denied fears and feelings about their failure to keep the corporation healthy could be blocking the team's problem-solving abilities *(denied emotions under-the-table)*.

3. Perhaps the executives don't have the knowledge or skills to solve the downsizing problem, but can't admit they don't know because in a top-down culture they are expected to have all the answers *(denied doubts about competence kept under-the-table)*.

4. The executives assume there will eventually be a win-lose political fight over what cuts are made and no one wants to say much in order to protect their turf *(denied politics kept under-the-table)*.

5. Given the paternalistic culture of Alpha, the executive team is like a family with a parent and children. Unconscious anger at the CEO for not taking care of them and the workforce is being repressed and acted out through avoidance or passive-aggressive behavior *(repressed feelings in the subconscious)*.

6. Norms of rational problem-solving are preventing the executive team from giving voice to creative or inspirational ideas about how to turn the situation around. Team members are afraid to raise such ideas for fear of being laughed at as out-of-touch dreamers *(unexpressed possibilities hiding above-the-clouds)*.

It goes without saying that more information about the executive team and the current context, patterns, and emphases or omissions would help to narrow the list of hunches. Usually it is useful to generate more than one plausible hunch and then seek additional information, clues, and insights to narrow your focus. In the end, you can't always be sure you know exactly what is going on covertly, but you may be pretty sure something meaningful is hidden. You can, however, develop some well-educated hunches to guide actions that could help move things along. Your initial actions will also generate additional information to refine and better target your hunches and actions.

In the Alpha case, for example, one reasonable hunch is that denied emotions are blocking problem-solving in the executive committee. Thus, taking some actions to allow fears and concerns to be expressed in some acceptable way could be a reasonable first step. Asking people to spend a little time in small subgroups, sharing their hopes and fears about the crisis, could free up their thinking. If this produces clear results, additional actions in the same vein might be pursued. If not, it may be because expressing feelings of fear and

(continues)

(continued)

failure are still considered inappropriate. It could also mean your hunch is off target. It would then be appropriate to test another approach or hunch.

In diagnosing covert processes it's not about being right (correctly guessing what is hidden) but about developing guided judgments on the best possible actions to pursue to get overt engagement of important topics. The essence of the approach is to try something based on a good hunch and then see how the focal system responds. In short, do not act blindly, nor be blind to acting, when dealing with covert dynamics.

Covert Issues in Work Groups

In my experience, things that are overt in work groups tend to be task-related, rational, and defined by the prevailing group norms as legitimate and appropriate in the context. If asked, most members of the group would be aware of and could describe "what is going on." On the other hand, covert processes are more often relationship-related, emotionally based, often out-of-awareness or unconscious, and defined by the group norms as illegitimate or inappropriate. If asked, some group members might have a sense that something is going on that they can't quite put their finger on, or that something is not being expressed, while others might not be aware of anything out of the ordinary. Some typical covert issues in work groups include:

- Feelings, emotions, and needs regarding power, inclusion, authority, intimacy, attraction, trust, or anger.
- Fears, taboos, conflicts, and disagreements.
- Aspirations, hopes, dreams, or spiritual values that are considered too far out or pie-in-the-sky.
- Beliefs, norms, and cultural assumptions that guide and limit possibilities.
- Unconscious dynamics such as projection, transference, denial, compensation, and group-based psychodynamics.
- Deals, arrangements, understandings, and "politics" intended to advantage some over others.

- Professional and personal biases and prejudices.

- Unaddressed or unacknowledged differences based on culture, religion, gender, race, sexual orientation, physical ability, or styles.

- Formal and informal frameworks that are guiding thought and action, such as paradigms, theories, and "lessons learned."

Paying attention to a few areas of inquiry, oriented to the Covert Processes Model, can be a useful way to think about and look for hidden dynamics in work groups and teams. A worksheet version of the Covert Processes Model that can be used in work group diagnosis is shown in the accompanying illustration. This worksheet leaves out consideration of the possible effects of unconscious dynamics. Speculation about psychodynamics can certainly be added, however, if you and the work group are comfortable looking at those possibilities. Let's now look at each element of the model with a focus on diagnosis of possible hidden dynamics in work groups and teams.

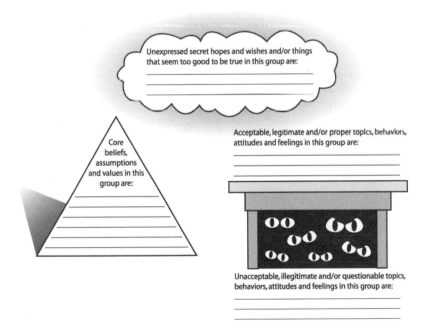

The Covert Processes Model Worksheet. © 1994 Marshak & Katz.

What's the Context?

To begin to understand what is going on in a group, it is helpful to have an understanding of the context that frames the situation. This includes the group's field of experience as well as its purpose, phase of development, and operating procedures. Knowing that a group of people has assembled to figure out how to downsize an organization rather than develop a new vision statement is a prerequisite for understanding what may be considered legitimate and appropriate behavior in the context.

What's On-the-Table?

What topics, behaviors, attitudes and or feelings are legitimate, proper, acceptable, and/or reasonable for discussion or attention by the group? You can get a sense of this by noting what gets addressed and stays addressed by group members. You might also pay attention to what gets raised and routinely put on-the-table. Parenthetically, you should also note what gets raised and routinely "knocked off the table." Remember, when something relevant to the group accomplishing its work is not on-the-table, or routinely gets knocked off the table, it is a signal that there is a covert dynamic at work.

What's Under-the-Table?

What topics, behaviors, attitudes and feelings are unacceptable, illegitimate, improper or questionable for discussion or attention by the group? You might ask yourself questions like the following: *What emotions, thoughts, fears, or needs might appropriately be present, but somehow never get raised or are quickly denied? What comes up routinely in other groups you've worked with, but not this one? What are some thoughts and feelings you think people might normally have in this situation, but somehow are not being expressed?*

What's Above-the-Clouds?

What topics, behaviors, attitudes and feelings are "too good to be true" and therefore hidden in this group? What secret hopes and wishes might reasonably be present—such as aspirations for greatness—but are not being expressed? What topics or behaviors get ridiculed as "too far out" or "airy-fairy" and then are quickly dropped? Remember, people will hide and conceal their valuables as well as their vulnerabilities and vices.

What's in the Prism?

Actions and behaviors that seem illogical or counterproductive to an outside observer may in fact be completely logical from the frame of reference of the group's prism. In fact, if we assume that most people are trying the best they can, then we have a powerful way to deduce what the contents of their prism may be. We simply ask ourselves: "What beliefs or assumptions would have to be in this group's prism for them to intentionally behave or act in this way?"

Another way to find out what is in the prism is to reflect on the question: "This group is behaving *as if* its guiding assumptions or beliefs are telling it that _____." Always keep in mind the meaning of anything is filtered through a prism. What may at first strike you as counterproductive could make complete sense through the group's prism. You may think people should directly address falling sales figures. From their prism, however, they may know that speaking out will make someone angry, and it is safer to avoid the topic. You might still need to address the avoidance behavior, but your actions are more likely to be successful when guided by solid hunches about the governing beliefs and assumptions in the group's prism.

What's in the Unconscious?

Looking for covert processes in a group's unconscious is not something we normally do, unless we are therapists or personal growth group facilitators. Consequently this is an area of covert processes that might be inappropriate for you to explore in any depth unless you have adequate training and the group's consent. Nonetheless, some of the more common manifestations of unconscious dynamics in groups (and individuals) can be identified. These provide clues about what to look for that most people can consider in the workplace setting.

Keep in mind, however, that the purpose of identifying unconscious dynamics is not to work them therapeutically. Instead, we seek to understand them in order to make better choices about our actions. Usually the simplest and most appropriate actions are to (1) recognize that you may be dealing with issues not amenable to rational problem-solving, and then (2) see if you can help make the group or focal system more aware of what might be going on. In other words, see if the issue(s) can be put on-the-table and engaged once brought to awareness. Some manifestations of unconscious dynamics include:

- **Projection,** where unacceptable aspects of a person or the group are attributed to another person or group. This is a way our unconscious protects us from having to confront something about ourselves that would make us anxious. Often what a team complains about in other groups or other levels of the organization are just as applicable to itself. When you hear what a group is saying about someone else, ask yourself how it might apply to them.

- **Transference,** where a current situation or person is perceived and responded to in ways that are based not on present reality but on unresolved issues from someone's past. Sometimes leaders or powerful figures in a group are responded to *as if* they were someone's mother or father. If you see a reaction that seems unwarranted or out-of-place for the circumstances, consider transference.

- **Repression or denial,** where some feeling, need, or thought is strongly denied even as it gets expressed through some alternative (and disguised) means. Sexual attraction between members of a work group can be considered inappropriate, and therefore denied and repressed. The attraction may then be expressed in the form of sharp bantering, sarcasm, or competitive behavior between the individuals.

- **Compensation,** where some denied deficiency or fear is addressed through an indirect and sometimes contradictory means. Work teams operating in dangerous situations may take

unnecessary risks as a show of bravado to compensate for their
very real but denied fears.

- **Untapped abilities and synergies,** where *positive* talents,
  creativity, or spiritual dimensions are repressed, denied, or
  projected onto others. Some of our most positive attributes and
  abilities may be left untapped or unrealized in work situations.
  Ask yourself if there are some untapped abilities in individuals or
  groups who are insistent that they are not, for example, creative
  or innovative.

- **The group voice,** where a member of the group expresses a
  thought, feeling, or need, seemingly for themselves, but in
  reality representing the collective unconscious of the group. In
  the Tavistock approach to group dynamics, it is assumed that
  group members play covert roles by expressing denied issues
  held by all or most members of the group (Banet and Hayden,
  1977). When someone says something that especially rings true,
  wonder whether it is covertly an issue for the whole group. The
  Tavistock school explicitly uses the term *covert processes* to
  refer to unconscious dynamics in groups. The present discussion
  includes this orientation, but takes a more encompassing view of
  covert processes.

- **Symbolic expressions,** where an unconscious dynamic is expressed through such means as a vivid word image, seating arrangement, drawing, or tune someone is humming. Sometimes
  a cigar is just a cigar and sometimes it is symbolically something
  else. If people in a work group talk about being *brutally* honest
  with each other, you might legitimately wonder what the unspoken beliefs are about what complete honesty does to people.
  This dimension of developing hunches about covert processes
  will be discussed in more detail in the next chapter on symbolic
  diagnosis.

These are some of the cues and clues to consider as you explore
the covert dimensions of group dynamics. Clearly there is a lot more
going on in a group than the overt task and process! In the beginning

it may be helpful to start by focusing on only one or two covert aspects and then add more as this way of thinking becomes natural. You could begin by wondering what is under-the-table and above-the-clouds. As you become more practiced, you can add speculation about prism contents or unconscious dynamics.

Conclusion

Given the impact of covert dynamics on organizational change, it is important to develop your abilities to notice and generate hunches about what is missing, not said, or not expressed. These abilities are increasingly important as the scope, complexity, and rate of change escalates in today's organizations.

To develop these abilities requires you to do two things. First, you need to learn how to notice what is over- or under-emphasized in a specific situation. Second, you need to be able to develop alternative hunches about what is going on, considering the full range of possible covert processes that could be at work.

You may also need to do some self-reflection to see if there are any types of covert processes—for example, denied anger—with which you are uncomfortable or unpracticed.

CHAPTER 4

Decoding Subconscious Expressions

Noting emphases and omissions in expected patterns is an important way to develop clues about covert dynamics. Another way to recognize hidden dynamics—especially unconscious or out-of-awareness dynamics—is to pay attention to symbolic expressions such as word images (Marshak and Katz, 1992). Someone says to you, "We're dead in the water and going down. Soon it will be everyone for himself." You may hear this as a colorful statement that things are getting difficult, but you can also hear it as a symbolic expression that the ship is sinking!

If this person is looking at things through a sinking ship image in their prism, they may display the emotions and actions of someone on a sinking ship. The sinking ship imagery could be a symbolic message from the person's unconscious that is trying to communicate the seriousness of a situation otherwise being consciously denied: *Oh, things aren't that bad. No need to rush.*

Developing your ability to pay attention to symbolic clues will enhance your effectiveness in diagnosing covert processes. I found that my diagnostic insights increased dramatically once I allowed myself to recognize information that was in plain sight but was being conveyed through various symbolic modalities.

Symbolic Communication

Learning to work with the symbolic aspects of diagnosis involves two essential elements. First is a willingness to trust that symbolic expressions convey real information that otherwise might not be openly expressed; second is the learned ability to pay attention to both literal and symbolic communication simultaneously. The process of symbolic diagnosis is guided by four key premises and an overriding diagnostic principle. The four key premises are:

1. **Communication is literal and symbolic.** All communication is expressed through multiple modalities. All messages contain literal, conscious components as well as symbolic dimensions that may be out-of-awareness, as in the sinking ship example. Furthermore, communications may be verbal or nonverbal in nature, so we note how people act as well as what they say.

2. **Symbolic messages convey legitimate information.** Information conveyed through symbolic expression communicates real and legitimate issues, hopes, and concerns, the same as information conveyed through literal language.

3. **Symbolic messages may come from the unconscious.** Symbolic communication is the language of the unconscious. It sometimes provides a way to express things about which we may not be consciously aware, or which we may not be able to express analytically or literally.

4. **Symbolic messages may bypass conscious censorship.** People "know" more than what is in their conscious minds. They often communicate what is important to them symbolically, regardless of what they say they think. In that sense, symbolic messages may provide a channel of communication independent of what our conscious minds tell us should, or should not, be said.

With these four premises serving as a constant reminder to pay attention to the symbolic aspects of communications, a paradoxical principle informs the diagnostic process: **Explore literal messages symbolically and symbolic messages literally.**

These four premises plus the guiding principle tell us that the diagnosis of covert processes benefits from paying attention to the multiple meanings being expressed in a single communication. As will become clear in the discussions that follow, it also means occasionally being willing to engage in playful or intuitive ways of seeing, listening, and interpreting things.

Explore the Literal Symbolically

When diagnosing covert processes, we pay attention to literal communications for possible symbolic messages. Sometimes people send—possibly from their unconscious—a coded message that is highly important, but disguised as a literal statement. If we look at the literal message symbolically, we might be able to discover some useful, but previously covert, information.

Suppose people in a work group tell you: *You can't tell the truth around here because too many people would get hurt. You can tell the boss the truth, but only if you are willing to take your lumps.* Or, *We need to be brutally honest.* You could understand that, in their work group, telling the truth is difficult and painful. If you are on the alert for covert processes, it might also be appropriate to speculate about what is being communicated symbolically. What implicit or unconscious image would lead people to describe telling the truth in such a way? More specifically, what symbolic image of truth would lead to such statements? At a symbolic level, these people are talking as if truth is *what*?

In this work group, it is reasonable to wonder if people are symbolically experiencing truth as a weapon, or honesty as brutality. If so, what are the implications of that message? It would be difficult to imagine much honesty in a work setting that consistently evokes such strong images and feelings. Notice that, if you ask directly whether people think truth is a weapon that is used to brutalize people in their work group, it is possible the answer put on-the-table would be "no." It could be too dangerous to tell the truth about telling the truth! However, their unconscious may be revealing the truth symbolically.

Explore the Symbolic Literally

When symbolic expressions—*This office is like a prison!*—are examined for their literal as well as symbolic meanings, a wider range of diagnostic speculation becomes available. If someone makes the offhand comment "This office is like a prison!" it can be heard as a symbolic way of expressing the feelings and thoughts they have about their workplace. The individual may be conveying a sense of restriction, confinement, isolation, punishment, or surveillance.

Taking the symbolic statement literally would suggest responding to the comment as if the person were actually in prison. Appropriate diagnostic follow-up could include: *How exactly is this place like a prison? What type of prison is it? Who are the inmates, the guards, and the warden? Why are you here? When are you due to get out?* These and other questions can expand your understanding of the original jail metaphor. And, based on our premises, you could assume that some part of the person feels as if they are in prison and is stating that "fact."

To understand the full range of data available to you in diagnosing covert processes, it is clear that you need to tune yourself to hear, see, and experience both the literal and symbolic dimensions of communication. Keep in mind that symbolic diagnosis is always used in conjunction with other data-gathering approaches to develop hunches and *not* firm conclusions. In the preceding example about telling the truth, the significance of the comments must be evaluated in the context of other available information. That said, valuable diagnostic hunches can arise from paying attention to both literal and symbolic communications.

Four Major Modalities (The 4 M's)

Tuning into symbolic communications involves paying attention to multiple sources of data, including sights, sounds, feelings, and movement. Because information is being sent both literally and symbolically, you must be prepared to understand it both literally and symbolically. There are four dominant ways symbolic information is expressed. For purposes of alliteration they are defined here as the "4 M's" of metaphor, music, movement and media (see table). As we look at each of these modalities, keep in mind that to find the clues provided by symbolic expression you must learn to listen, look, feel, and experience *between the lines* of literal meaning.

The 4 M's of Symbolic Communication

Metaphor	Music	Movement	Media
Figures of speech, similes, stories, parables, myths, and word imagery (e.g., noticing that people are saying things like "This place is a prison.")	Voice, tone, tempo, volume, speed, rhythm, harmony, beat, tune, and themes in song or music (e.g., noticing that the voices in a team meeting sound like a "funeral march.")	Gestures, facial cues, posture, position, stance, spatial relations, and body language (e.g., noticing people with opposing views are somehow sitting opposite each other at the table.)	Pictures, paintings, drawings, photography, and other representational media (e.g., noticing someone important was left out of an informally drawn organization chart.)

Metaphor

The category of metaphor includes figures of speech, similes, stories, parables, myths, and word imagery. Although the mode of expression is through language, the focus is on the symbolic meaning or image that is painted verbally:

- Do people describe their work group as: A family? A football team? A circus? A feudal system?

- Is the workplace described as: Sink or swim? May the best man win? Only the strong survive? Walking on eggshells? Being on thin ice? Dancing around the issues?

As you watch or listen to people at a meeting what metaphors or images come to mind? Do they seem repetitive? Are they going around in circles? Like kids on a play station? Are they moving full steam ahead with everyone on the right track?

Do certain themes or expressions occur regularly in discussions? *We have to take the offensive. Their side is out to get us. Send an advance scouting party to see what they are up to. We can't afford to win the battle and lose the war.* Or, with respect to the truth: *It's hard to tell the truth. The facts can be cruel. Honesty hurts,* in contrast to *The truth is freeing. Facts are our friends. Honesty helps.*

What might any of these word images tell you about possible covert processes in the focal system if they were somehow literally true?

Music

The category of music includes all forms of auditory expression: voice, tone, tempo, volume, speed, rhythm, harmony, beat, tune, as well as themes in song and music. Examples:

- As you listen to a team, do their discussions sound like: An orchestra? A jazz band? A string quartet? A reggae group? Rap?

- Are all voices: In tune? Heard? In harmony? Dissonant? Shrill? Soothing? Sharp? Flat?

- Is the rhythm of the team fast or slow? Is everyone in the same rhythm? What's the beat? The pace? The tempo?

- As you listen to the team's discussions do you hear: A funeral march? A joyful tune? A melancholy refrain? A wedding march?

If you were to pick any song or musical selection that might best capture your impression of the team and its deliberations, what would it be? If you were asked to compose the theme song to their work, how would it sound? What might any of these musical messages tell you about possible covert processes in the focal system if they were somehow literally true?

Movement

This category includes all forms of kinesthetic expression: gestures, facial cues, posture, position, spatial relations, and body language. Things to consider include:

- How are people sitting or standing? Are key people sitting in opposition to one another? Lined up in support? How close or far apart are they? Are they looking down? Looking up? Are individuals or subgroups sitting together? Apart? Scattered? How have they positioned themselves?

- Do people touch one another? Shake hands? Hug? Avoid contact? What does their posture and positioning convey? Warmth? Distance? Comfort? Formality?

- Do gestures and body language seem to display openness and support or displeasure and opposition? Do people look confused? Angry? Perplexed? Bored? Turned on or turned off?

Based on your observations, how would you describe the movement or dance of the focal system? Is everyone in step? Moving at a snail's pace? Frolicking? Jumping? Dragging their feet? Are they moving in circles? Are they taking three steps forward and one step back? If any of these kinesthetic expressions were literally true, what might that tell you about possible covert processes in the focal system?

Media

The category of media includes: pictures, paintings, drawings, photography, and other representational media. This category also includes forms of graphic representation such as organization charts. Examples:

- If you were to take a snapshot of a work group at a given moment in time, is anything or anyone missing from the picture? Are certain aspects, topics, or dimensions over-emphasized? Minimized?

- When you look at the organization's logo, brochures, reports, presentations, and graphics, do they suggest an organization that is lined up? Boxed in? A network? Squared away? Disconnected? Clear or fuzzy? Open-ended? Two-dimensional? Unclear about the present or future?

- If someone shows you, or especially draws for you, an organization chart, which units or divisions seem most central? Which are peripheral? Is anyone or anything left out of the picture? Who's on top? Who has to "go through" who to get to the top? Are the work units on different sides of the chart in opposition or competition with each other? Does the chart look clear? Cluttered? Confusing?

- If you were to draw a picture symbolically capturing what is going on in the focal system, what might you draw? What would be the key themes and representations? What would your picture lead you to think and how would it make you feel? If any of these visual representations were literally true, what might that tell you about possible covert processes in the focal system?

The 4 M's in Action

The following vignettes drawn from real-life experiences are examples of symbolic communications in the context of organizational change efforts.

Metaphor in Action

During a planning meeting of a task force charged with designing and implementing a new way of doing business that would ultimately impact the existing organization structure, reward system, information systems, and career paths, certain phrases kept coming up throughout the discussion from different members of the task force: *If it ain't broke, don't fix it. Remember, we have to minimize downtime and get this up and running as soon as possible. Maybe we only need to tinker with this to make it work. That's been running well for ten years, I don't see why we need to fix it now.*

One member of the task force picked up on these phrases and began listening for what was being expressed at a more symbolic level. From the statements it appeared that task force members were operating from an implicit shared metaphor that the organization was some kind of machine. Their discussions seemed to focus on making small incremental changes (tinkering), rather than the fundamental and transformational shifts called for by the situation.

Playing the hunch that the task force was covertly constrained by an unexpressed limiting belief (*We are here to fix the machine*), an explicit change in metaphor was suggested: *You know, maybe what we are designing is a fundamentally new model of the organization that incorporates the latest technology and achieves higher performance standards.* The invitation to think in terms of designing a higher-performance machine rather than repairing an old outdated one was appealing and members of the task force began to see their assignment in a new way. They began talking about fundamental changes in aspects of the organization they had not considered earlier because those aspects were still functioning and it had been assumed they didn't need fixing.

Music in Action

During an executive planning session to consider organizational changes in response to a dramatically altered competitive situation, the discussion kept getting bogged down as people debated how much change was really needed and how different changes would or would not help the business. During a break one of the executives noticed that another executive was humming a tune and asked what it was. The response: "The theme song of *Gone With the Wind* keeps playing in my head."

When asked what that might mean, the executive paused for a moment, then smiled and said, "As the movie opens, the theme song plays under an introductory narrative that ends with the words, '. . . And an entire way of life was gone with the wind.'" The image of drastic change struck a chord in both executives. They shared their concerns about the impacts of the changes they were planning. Following the break they told the rest of the group what they had talked about.

Soon the entire executive group started relating their fears about how drastic the changes might have to be, and what that would mean to everyone in the organization who was used to the old way of doing things. They also talked about whether people would see them as having failed, letting them down by not preserving the organization as it had always been. The planning session became the most intense they had ever had on the subject of organizational change.

Movement in Action

During a team-building session with a group of men and women, one of the men got up and said "I want to make a point." He then moved a flip chart so that it blocked the view of the team leader and then walked to stand on the same side of the room as the rest of the men, looking down at the women. The human resources consultant didn't miss the symbolic message. Later in the session, after more safety had been established, the man revealed his "secret": "Sometimes I feel more comfortable with the men on the team than the women, and sometimes I feel competitive with our team leader." Obviously, this message had already been conveyed through his kinesthetic symbolic communication. He made more than one kind of point when he got up to move the flip chart!

Media in Action

During a meeting to implement a new organizational vision, middle managers drew pictures representing what the organization and its people would look like when the new vision was fully implemented. After managers described their pictures, the consultant asked why some of the people were pictured with no eyes while others had eyes. The initial response: *Because we are poor artists.* However, as the consultant gently continued to explore the identity of the people with no eyes, a somewhat hesitant response was: *Top management.* When asked about the people who had eyes: *The rest of the organization, especially the people in this room.*

This opened the way for a candid discussion of the managers' perceptions and feelings about the leadership of top management: *They are blind to what's really going on around here. It's the blind men describing the elephant, but we're the ones who end up having to take care of it. They have walked into this vision thing with their heads down and eyes shut; they don't know what they have gotten us into.*

They have their heads in a cloud and can't see the road ahead of us; we are going to crash!

Once the deep mistrust of top leadership had surfaced and been discussed, it was much easier to begin a rational discussion of the new vision's merits and potential problems. The managers began to talk about why the new vision might be needed and how it might make a positive difference. The meeting concluded with a decision to seek a face-to-face meeting with top management to discuss the best way to achieve the new vision, to gain a better understanding of the view from the top, and perhaps to "open their eyes a little."

The following case illustrates how symbolic information may turn up during a change project as an adjunct to overt information. It also shows how symbolic information can provide an early signal about a central theme or issue.

Smith-Jones Corporation

Smith-Jones was a leading corporation in its industry. People who worked for Smith-Jones generally spoke highly of the corporation and its senior leaders, although they would occasionally imply that there were "some interesting dynamics at the top" without going into details. If pressed to say more, people simply said that things at Smith-Jones were no different than anyplace else, and maybe better.

The Initial Meeting

I was invited to come to a meeting with Pat, Smith-Jones' executive vice president of administration. At the time I had not previously worked with the organization or with Pat. After opening pleasantries, Pat said they wanted to explore team development with Peter's (the CEO) top team, of which Pat was a member. When I asked about desired outcomes the response was "We need to work better together." When I asked for more specifics, Pat responded, "We're too siloed, there's not enough trust, we avoid conflict, and agreements made in meetings are afterwards reversed in the hallway."

When asked who would be participating, Pat replied that it would be all

(continues)

(continued)

direct reports of the CEO. Listening closely, I did not hear the name of Paul, the COO, nor were any of the functions or activities mentioned that are most closely associated with a chief operating officer. When I asked about Paul, the response was, "He's not a member of the team and won't be attending."

This puzzled me because, based on the pattern I had observed in many other organizations, Paul as COO would report directly to Peter, the CEO. When I asked again about Paul, I got a look of exasperation and the comment, "He has his own team; we don't cross that line. Let's get back to talking about team development for the CEO's top team." Curious now, I asked if Pat could draw an organization chart of the CEO's team, indicating who would be involved in the development work.

On a whiteboard Pat drew a picture of five or six people, but they did not include the COO, nor did the picture include some other functions usually associated with corporate headquarters. I then asked if Pat could show me where Paul was located. In response, Pat drew in Paul in a way that made him parallel to Peter and with no line connecting the two of them. This was a picture of two independent and parallel executives, as if they were running separate organizations. When I inquired about the functions not represented in the picture, Pat said they were part of Paul's camp and would not be involved in the team development.

What did Pat mean by "Paul's camp"? "Well, there is Peter's camp and there is Paul's camp. The team development would be for the people in Peter's camp." What would happen if Paul or any of the people in his camp were to become part of the team development activity? Pulling back, in what I assumed at the time was disbelief or surprise, Pat said that would never happen because there was no real communication or trust between members of the two camps. Besides, Paul and his people were very aggressive and always looking for ways to encroach on "our" territory. In fact, one of the reasons for the desired team development was to work on their solidarity so they could be better armed to deal with Paul and "his organization."

My final question at this point: "Pat, you are EVP of administration. How do you deal with Paul as COO?" Pat's response, although anticipated, still surprised me. "I don't deal with him directly at all. We have a very combative relationship. He won't attend any of the meetings called by people in Peter's camp. Besides, I deal with Peter, and he prefers that the people in his camp deal with him and not the people in the other camp."

Early Indicators and Hunches

At this point I thought I had heard enough, both literally and symbolically, to offer my thoughts on Pat's proposal. I wondered aloud how the executives were going to address the leadership issues for Smith-Jones if they continued working in two separate camps. I went on to ask if the most difficult issues of silos, low trust, conflict avoidance, and hallway reversals happened within each of the camps or only between the two camps. After a moment of reflection Pat said it was clearly between the two camps.

Finally, I wondered if someone could talk with the CEO about team development that would involve all of the top executives. "I'm not sure, I'll have to check with Peter." The meeting then ended. On the way out, Pat smiled and said, "Let's see what happens next." At that point I left, assuming it was at best a fifty-fifty proposition I would get a call back.

Continuing Data and Dynamics

I never did work with Pat or Peter, and the proposed team development event never happened. Over the years I consulted occasionally at Smith-Jones, noticing the various training initiatives to enhance collaboration, hearing people talk about how decisions would get changed later, and listening as various staff complained about how hard it was to get the executives on the same page. They all want things their own way, and staff had to engage in shuttle diplomacy, going back and forth to get even temporary agreements on anything.

There was even a reorganization of some executive responsibilities between Peter and Paul "to improve coordination and efficiency of operations." The relationship between Peter and Paul was never addressed and rarely talked about. If it did come up, people quickly changed the subject or commented that things weren't so bad. Once, Pat asked me what I thought would be needed to make the culture of Smith-Jones less siloed and more collaborative.

(continues)

(continued)

My brief answer was that, until the relationship between Peter and Paul was addressed and resolved appropriately, the culture was not going to change. Their rivalry was at the core of everything. It modeled—and encouraged—the behaviors that were occurring throughout the organization. Pat replied that nothing could be done about their relationship unless the board did something, and that wasn't going to happen. "I guess you have your answer," I replied.

Coda

Several years after my comment to Pat, the company began to experience poor results. This was at least partly due to a lack of communication and collaboration between Peter and Paul, and among key departments and executives. Both Peter and Paul left the company and a completely new executive team was put in place. One of the first priorities of the new CEO was to initiate actions and programs to foster more collaboration and direct communication throughout the company.

Comments

This case presents several important lessons. First, symbolic information can provide essential clues, or corroborating information, about covert dynamics. In the case as presented, the symbolic data may seem obvious. I can assure you, however, that until I began to take symbolic expressions seriously I would have missed most of it. Second, noticing symbolic themes early on can lead to questions and inquiries that may reveal critical information not initially presented or considered relevant. Third, in some cases there are covert processes you won't be able to address, at least immediately. This may be true even if you know exactly what they are. In those instances, you work on what is really needed, and not on things that are off-target or ill-conceived, like team development for *half* an executive team. In time, through your efforts or the efforts of others, the situation may change enough to allow the issues to be put on-the-table and engaged in constructive ways.

Symbolic Diagnosis Reminders

Finally, here are some reminders when working with symbolic data for purposes of developing hunches about covert dynamics:

- Covert blocking factors are often presented openly in a symbolic way through one or more people in a focal system.

- Noticing symbolic messages gives you important insights to guide further diagnosis and action.

- Significant movement can occur when you recognize symbolic messages as an unspoken invitation to address the issues they raise.

- Addressing the theme(s) of a symbolic message is not an end unto itself, but a way to attend to covert dynamics that may be impacting performance.

Conclusion

When you allow yourself to pay attention to symbolic modes of expression you will find a wealth of previously ignored information. Hearing someone humming a tune, as in the *Gone with the Wind* example, can provide as much information for exploring issues and concerns as the overt statement "I'm afraid we could lose everything in this change." Because symbolic expressions provide a link between our unconscious and conscious minds, they provide a bridge between what is censored and what is openly discussed. Finally, it is crucial to remember that your role is not that of a mind reader probing for conclusions about the covert issues in a focal system. Nor is it one of confronting focal system members with hidden truths and then walking away. The purpose of symbolic diagnosis is to facilitate a process of discovery within the focal system. Never play "gotcha!"

CHAPTER 5

▶ # Five Basic Keys

Clearly, organizational change can be thwarted by the fears, untested assumptions, unconscious reactions, and under-the-table dealings of its members. Yet change can be facilitated by unleashing hidden creativity, removing unspoken blocks, altering mindsets, and giving voice to "unspeakable" visions of greatness. To prepare for dealing with hidden dynamics, this chapter presents five keys for engaging covert processes. I have found these basic building blocks to be essential. If I neglect to follow them carefully, I am much less effective. The five basic keys are:

1. Create a safe environment.

2. Be selective and seek movement, not exposure.

3. Assume people are trying their best.

4. Look in the mirror.

5. Act consistent with expectations of you and your role.

Key 1: Create a Safe Environment

First and foremost, in all work with covert processes, is to establish enough psychological safety to allow hidden dynamics to be revealed.

It's worth noting that early meanings of the word *covert* included "sheltered" and "protected." In those meanings of the word, covert processes exist to protect against the risks associated with putting something on-the-table that is considered to be inappropriate, illegitimate, or unacceptable. Perfect safety is too high a standard, but "safe enough" for people to put things on-the-table and openly engage them is the prime directive of covert processes work.

Fear and Threat

The Covert Processes Model tells us that things are on-the-table when the contents of the guiding prism(s) interpret them to be legitimate, proper, and acceptable, unless they are unconscious or out-of-awareness. If they are perceived to be too good to be true or questionable, illegitimate, or unacceptable, they will be knocked off or kept off the table. Most people try consciously to avoid saying or doing things that the prevailing norms and beliefs find questionable or unacceptable. To do otherwise is to court redress, sanctions, embarrassment, or worse. Fear or threat of repercussions is a major reason things become covert and are kept off-the-table.

Psychological Safety

It is essential to create a psychologically safe environment in order to address covert processes. Keep in mind that things will be hidden when people feel there is a risk of exposure. Putting someone on the spot in a team meeting by accusing them of being too emotional is likely to elicit a denial: *No! I am not angry, hurt, jealous, afraid!* Questioning someone's competence in front of others will do the same: *No, I did not make a mistake, fail to follow through, screw up!*

It's not that you can't address these topics, but you must address them in ways that are perceived as safe enough for open exploration. Remember that safety is always in the eye (prism) of the beholder. In short, all types of emotions, thoughts, needs, motives—and even hopes, dreams, and wishes—will remain hidden until people feel safe enough to reveal them. Therefore, the primary intervention in all work with covert processes is to create a safe enough environment for further inquiry. To create a psychologically safe environment requires at a minimum that you establish trust, boundaries, and a sense of control in the focal system.

Establish Trust

Creating a safe environment means establishing a context where people feel there is trust. People will not reveal their secret hopes and dreams, nor their doubts and misgivings, if they believe the information will be used against them, hold them up to ridicule, punish them, put them down, embarrass them, or cause them to suffer some other negative repercussion. They must trust that what is shared will be treated with care and respect. They must trust they will not suffer retribution for letting the cat out of the bag. They must trust that what they put on-the-table will be used toward important and meaningful ends, not simply to satisfy your curiosity.

This means that a work setting where snide comments, put-downs, jokes at others' expense, studied cynicism, fear of retribution, one-upmanship, and gossip are the norm will be one where covert processes flourish. You must do whatever you can to create a climate of sincerity, respect, inquiry, trust, and collaboration.

Establish Sense of Control

People need to feel that they have some control over how much to reveal, when, in what way, and in what depth. An environment where people feel they will be forced or bullied is an environment with a lot of covert processes.

You need to create ways of addressing covert issues that make clear there are boundaries and limits to what will happen. For example, you can establish ground rules, time limits, and clear steps and processes and then pointedly stick to them. You also need to make clear that people will have the ability to control the pace, process, and purpose(s) of any interactions. All of these and more are important aspects of helping to set an environment where people feel safe enough to put things on-the-table.

Threat in Eye of Beholder

Keep in mind the intent of most covert processes, such as denial and repression, is to protect the focal system from real or perceived threat. While an outside observer might not see a situation as dangerous, you must remember that the focal system is operating from its own frame of reference. What is dangerous is *always* defined by the focal system's belief system, not yours.

Pay attention to the particular methods and behaviors used by the focal system to guard against perceived danger. These indicate when something might be threatening, and signal the types of defenses used by the focal system to protect against threat. For example, an elaborate process of sign-offs and pre-meetings before anything is discussed in an executive group may be an indicator that open discussion of new topics is covertly threatening. Observing that process, you might be able to speculate about the governing prism beliefs and what you might do to create enough safety for more spontaneous interactions (should that be desired).

Avoid Becoming the Threat

If you act from your own frame of reference without much attention to the focal system's prism, you are likely to be perceived as blind to the realities, or foolhardy. Naturally, this makes you and your actions dangerous. When you ignore the focal system's perspective about what is dangerous, you risk violating the primary condition of safety; instead, your actions must recognize the sense of threat to the focal system inherent in revealing what has been previously hidden.

You might find that people in a team meeting are more willing to report small-group discussions of concerns rather than individual expressions. As an outsider working with a focal system, you must understand that generally members of the focal system have a more accurate sense of what is threatening than you do. For example, expecting people to fear no retribution following a two-day teambuilding session may be unrealistic if the team's earlier experiences included retribution. Important information about what is really going on can be missed if you have a blind spot that always sees such behavior as "resistance to change" versus "protection from threat."

Key 2: Seek Movement not Exposure

The Covert Processes Model makes it clear that multiple covert processes are always present and that they result from a variety of complex dynamics. Covert processes are also based in many cases on the focal system protecting itself from anxiety and fear of exposure. This suggests that you must be selective in what you focus on and always mindful of safety. In being selective, keep in mind that the purpose of addressing a covert process is to facilitate desired movement, not to expose something or someone as an end in itself.

You need to be clear about desired outcomes and to focus on the covert dynamic(s) most directly related to preventing the focal system from achieving them. Always avoid raising issues that cannot be addressed or that are not ready to be addressed. Exposing someone or something may temporarily put something on-the-table, but may violate the necessary conditions for dealing with the hidden issues effectively. The following ideas are designed to help you be selective as you seek movement, not exposure.

Be Alert

You need to stay alert to the full range of covert processes that may be operating simultaneously in a focal system. This requires an acceptance that there will always be covert processes in any organizational change effort. It also requires you to have some covert process diagnostic skills, as well as clarity about your own prism, which may filter your perceptions of a situation. In other words, you need to guard against having your biases and preferences lead you to ignore certain covert dynamics. For example, if you are uncomfortable thinking politically, you may miss some important signals about power and politics in the focal system.

Be Nonjudgmental

It is important for you to maintain a stance of nonjudgmental inquiry about any covert processes you suspect are at work in a particular situation. Once you begin to judge, either positively or negatively, you may close off inquiry too quickly without staying open to all that may be going on: you have seen enough, reached a conclusion, and are ready to act. Worse, if you have judged the situation negatively, you may be tempted to attack or punish those involved, thereby violating the perceived safety of the situation: *It's really terrible what is going on and he/she/they deserve to be exposed. Well, Kim, I think if you really cared about this organization you would speak up about any misgivings. Leslie, that kind of statement is totally inappropriate given the seriousness of the situation we are facing, are you on-board or not?*

Instead, a stance of curiosity is needed. Wondering why something is happening and what covert processes may be involved will help keep you open: *I wonder what he/she/they think is risky or dangerous about this change? Kim, you've been quieter than usual—do you have anything to add? Leslie, will you say more, I'm not sure I fully understand what you mean.*

Clarify Desired Outcomes

To deal with covert processes effectively you must be clear about the outcomes you and the focal system seek to achieve. Do you want to break a log jam so that a decision can be made? Are you trying to get some important information onto the table to increase the quality of a decision? Do you want to find out a fuller range of the feelings people are experiencing in order to increase collaboration? Are you trying to encourage creativity to open up new possibilities?

Without clarity on what you intend to achieve, you risk revealing something just for the sake of doing it. Some people don't like the idea that anything is hidden or covert and confuse exposure with achieving desired results: *They are hiding something and I am going to expose them!* This might through happenstance create the desired effect, but it risks violating people's sense of safety over what is revealed and for what reasons. Being clear about desired outcomes helps you to focus on exactly what to address: *Hmm. We are trying to agree on the budget for this project and are making progress even though we haven't talked about all our implicit assumptions. I probably don't need to point that out right now.*

Avoid Exposure for Its Own Sake

Most people pay attention to body language and other cues about what others are really thinking and intending. The focal system will be sensitive to your intentions, no matter what you say publicly. Consequently, you need to be clear with yourself and with them that you are seeking progress, not punishment.

If people in the focal system suspect that you are likely to expose someone, without good cause or without safeguards, then trust will be low and little will be accomplished. Again, the key question is: Do you want to have the focal system move forward or do you want to expose, ridicule, blame, or otherwise "get" someone? Again, this does not mean that you can't confront or hold someone accountable, but the way it is done makes all the difference in the world.

Measure Success by Movement

Keeping in mind that you are trying to achieve movement towards an intended outcome, not exposure per se, is also important in measuring the effectiveness of your actions. If there is movement based on what you have done, then your actions can be interpreted as effective even if nothing covert was publicly revealed.

The same is not true if the purpose is to expose, regardless of movement. It does little good to reveal a secret if the focal system is not prepared to deal with it. Worse, the inability to deal with it could end up convincing everyone that they were right in keeping it a secret in the first place. Thus effectiveness in working with covert processes must be measured in terms of movement rather than degrees of exposure.

During a staff meeting two of my colleagues got into a heated disagreement. The room became tense because everyone knew they often argued with each other. People felt uncomfortable, and we were distracted from the work we had gathered to do. I wondered if the two debaters had gotten stuck in their arguments—that neither one could back off without thinking they had lost out to the other. Clearly this was not the time for anyone to point out their disruptive behavior or speculate on what was causing it. We needed them to join the rest of the team.

Acting on the hunch that neither one was willing to lose to the other in front of colleagues, I spoke up by summarizing what each had been saying and then acknowledging the important points each had made. I then suggested we all needed to think about their points over a break. My actions were not intended to ignore their behavior, but represented a calculated way to allow them to disengage, save face, and let some informal hallway chatter change the dynamics.

When we reconvened, they stopped arguing with each other and collaboratively joined the rest of us. In the long run, their disruptive interpersonal dynamics had to be addressed. In the short run, we needed movement. There was no point in pointing out their excessively competitive egos in a team setting where that was not likely to be successful.

Key 3: Assume People Are Trying Their Best

In working with covert processes it helps to proceed from the assumption that most people are trying their best. This means that the person or group is trying to be effective and do a good job, even when what they are doing is clearly not very effective or even competent. Working from the assumption that people are trying their best does three things that set the stage for effectively engaging covert dynamics.

Develop Hunches

The assumption that people are trying their best is important to developing hunches about the contents of the focal system's prism, even though you may not be able to access its contents directly. If you assume that people are trying their best then, regardless of the effectiveness of their actions, you can speculate about what might be guiding those actions. In short, you ask yourself the diagnostic question: What beliefs, assumptions, values, or theories would have to exist in their prism to lead them to behave in this way, assuming they are trying their best?

In this regard you are like an anthropologist plumbing the cultural beliefs that underlie a society's observed behaviors and customs. In short, you develop hunches about the contents of the prism by deducing the implied beliefs leading to observable behavior: *Everywhere I go in this organization they talk about referring things upstairs, or having to check with the boss, or running things up the flagpole. Do they have something in their prism about deferring to leaders?* This type of speculation tends to ensure that actions will be taken from the frame of reference of the focal system and not from an outside perspective. Working with the prism will be discussed further in Chapters 7 and 8.

Signal Your Support

When you assume that people are trying their best, you exhibit behaviors and attitudes that communicate that you believe the focal system is capable of changing itself. This is an invitation for people to take initiative rather than depending on others for leadership. Operating from this stance does not mean blindly accepting that the focal system is competent or wise. Coaching and developmental support may still be needed, but this support is less threatening than directly challenging people's abilities.

Empathy and Further Inquiry

The assumption that the focal system is trying its best encourages you to stay open to new information, empathize with the focal system, and invites inquiry rather than judgment. Adopting this stance creates a psychologically safer setting that is more conducive to disclosure and exploration than to defensiveness. Your demeanor will be markedly different if you assume that a focal system keeps bumping up against the same obstacle because of a blind spot in its prism, rather than because people are resistant, stupid, or acting politically.

Key 4: Look in the Mirror

To deal with covert processes successfully and responsibly, it is helpful to be continually aware of your own field of experience, prism, shadow needs, drives, and dynamics. This ensures that you are acting on issues in the focal system rather than addressing your own reflection in the mirror.

Be Self-Aware

If one of my covert processes is fear of conflict, how likely is it that I will try to engage unspoken or under-the-table conflict in a focal system? Total self-awareness about all of your covert processes is not possible—we all have our blind spots. However, whether you are a leader, staff specialist, or consultant, you have a professional responsibility to be as self-aware as possible. This is especially true when dealing with covert dynamics. Otherwise, you run the risk that your own covert processes may be distorting your observations or serving as the real motivation for your actions. Consider the following examples:

- You believe the focal system cannot change without your help because you have a (secret) need to be seen as a powerful helper. This leads to actions that keep people dependent on you rather than your helping them to develop their own abilities.

- You consistently choose to ignore angry exchanges because you are personally uncomfortable with anger and emotional displays. This may help keep the lid on things, but it prevents the focal system from dealing with important feelings and issues.

- You don't see how the larger system is impacting the specific situation because the primary theories and models you use to interpret events mostly address individual and group dynamics. For example, you tend to see an interdepartmental conflict as resulting from the personalities of the two managers rather than role conflict created by the organization structure.

- You convince a focal system to pursue a particular approach to a situation, allegedly to meet their needs, when in reality you are advocating it because you feel especially comfortable using that approach. For example, you advocate a strategic planning session when what is really needed is improved team relationships.

- You disguise or conceal gaps in your experience or competence because you want the opportunity to work on a particular project. As a result you get to work on the project, but you may not have the degree of experience or expertise needed.

Know What's You, What's Them

As previously mentioned, to reduce the potential of your own covert processes distorting perception and judgment it is helpful to have a high degree of personal awareness. We cannot get rid of all our own covert processes, but we can become aware enough to recognize when our own patterns are being reflected back to us from the focal system with which we are working. When I am aware of my own biases, hidden needs, and secret fears, I am in a better position to second-guess myself and am motivated to generate alternative hunches about what may be going on.

It can be useful, in working with covert processes, to collaborate with someone else. A colleague can help track the complexities of the covert processes in the focal system, provide another view through a different prism, and be a mirror if any of your "stuff" is being confused with their "stuff." Always be open to the possibility that the covert process blocking movement in a particular situation is your own. Perhaps you know that you have a tendency to question the value of corporate staffs. This is important to keep in mind if you end up working on a change project initiated by a corporate staff. Again, having a colleague to work with or confide in at such times can be invaluable and is certainly a situation where two heads are better than one.

Key 5: Act Consistent with Expectations

Knowing when and why to address possible covert dynamics can be just as difficult as knowing how to do it. Is it all right for you to put things on-the-table unilaterally when no one else is raising them? Should anything that is hidden or covert be put on-the-table, or just those things that are directly related to the specific purpose of the focal system at that moment? The following discussion provides some guidance on such questions.

Ensure Clear Understandings

First, you should take action only when the focal system wants or needs to engage a covert process and such actions are consistent with your role. Addressing anger issues arising from a manager's promotion may not be appropriate, especially if you are working with the manager's team to plan a ten-year celebration. No matter how clear the underlying issue may be to you, bringing such feelings out into the open could violate the necessary conditions of perceived safety when that was not an expectation of your role. At the same time, you must pay attention to the spirit as well as the specifics of your role. Are you a staff person asked to be involved because leaders need your help on the ten-year celebration or because they covertly want your help to become a better team? Remember that clear understandings and expectations are just as important when working with covert processes as with any other type of work.

Renegotiate Expectations

Another dimension of engaging covert processes introduces an additional level of judgment into decision making. Chapter 4 suggested that symbolic expressions, possibly from the focal system's unconscious, are important messages to heed. You may be asked overtly to help plan the ten-year celebration, but become aware of symbolic or indirect requests for help with suppressed anger and resentment. Someone might say "I feel as if we're getting ready to cook, but the lid is on too tight" while looking directly at you. Or perhaps there will be side inquiries about whether you have ever worked with a team where there was a lot of conflict. You need to pay attention to such indirect or symbolic messages; they could be coded signals requesting help.

At such times, it is appropriate for you to renegotiate expectations so you can respond to the coded messages without violating the focal system's understanding of why you are present. If you lack the necessary skills to help the team explore underlying issues, perhaps you can help them find someone who does. Renegotiations must be done clearly, with respect for the fact that the setting is not safe enough for the issue to be raised openly at that moment. Renegotiating expectations of your role also sends an important message: *I respect you and will not endanger you by acting without your knowledge or consent.*

As you begin exploring whether you will be able to pursue the coded requests for help, you must be establishing the climate of trust and safety that will be needed to address the covert issues effectively. This could be done, for example, by raising your observations or hunches privately with the team manager, seeing what response you get, and offering to help or to find help.

The following case applies the five basic keys to a change intervention involving the top executive team of a global company.

Comfort Foods

Comfort Foods was founded when three confectionary companies located in Europe and North America were merged into a holding company with two semi-autonomous operating divisions running the formerly independent companies. Major operations of manufacturing, sales, human resources, and finance were located in North America, Europe, and Asia. In addition, commodity and procurement operations were sited in South America, Africa, and Indonesia. The business of Comfort Foods was procuring and processing raw materials into bulk products that were then sold to global companies such as Nestlé and Unilever. Profitability of Comfort Foods quickly became a major concern due to high expenses, increased competition, and changing customer demands.

The Dream

Early on, Jose Patagonia, the South American–born president of Comfort Foods, had dreamed of one integrated global company rather than two mostly autonomous divisions. He believed that increased efficiencies and technology transfer would lead to higher profitability if all operations were integrated. Furthermore, Patagonia wanted to lead a great company and believed that would only be possible with complete integration. He wrote out his dream in a vision paper and distributed it to his team of executives based in North America and Europe. Nothing much happened after that. The team either avoided the topic or asked Patagonia for greater detail, which he was never able to provide to their satisfaction.

Behind the Scenes

Private conversations with each of the executives revealed some of what was going on. The heads of the two divisions, one based in North America

(continues)

(continued)

and the other in Europe, had run them as independent businesses before being merged into Comfort Foods. They were used to operating their own companies in their own way and did not buy into the merits of integration. Both division heads implied that only one of them could head up an integrated venture and neither believed that the president had the knowledge or temperament to lead such a venture. Both believed that their division and its methods of operation were superior and did not want to lose out to the other.

The other executives, who came from the merged companies or from prior associations with Jose Patagonia, were responsible for such functions as finance, commodity trading, marketing and sales, and human resources, and they had mixed feelings. All of them had some difficulty understanding the president's vision, and wondered how his dream might impact their responsibilities, positively or negatively. Each had old loyalties to the president or to one of the two division heads.

These functional executives were especially cautious in their comments because they were unsure who would emerge on top after an attempt at corporate integration. Patagonia himself was a bit uncertain about his dream because, while he believed in it passionately, he could not explain it well enough to get through to the other executives, especially the two heads of the divisions. He worried that he could not afford to have either one leave, and wondered out loud if his dream was practical.

Applying the Basics

Jose Patagonia asked me to lead a two-day retreat, hoping that his above-the-clouds dream could then be put on-the-table and realistically engaged by his team. In this case I will highlight elements that emerged during that event and relate them to the basic keys for engaging covert processes.

First, to help create a greater sense of psychological safety, the two-day retreat was announced as an "exploration of possibilities" rather than a decision-making meeting to avoid creating winners and losers. It was positioned as a limited step that would be followed by an assessment of what made sense to do next, including nothing at all. Having an outside consultant facilitate the meeting assured some that it would not get out of control and that no one person or position would dominate the discussions. Patagonia also felt more comfortable working with a consultant who might support him as he made the case for his dream. I interviewed everyone before the event to gather background information and begin establishing relationships of trust.

In planning the retreat, it was critical to decide what its focus would be. Many issues and covert dynamics presented themselves. These included questions of politics and trust among team members, fear of losing power or position, inability to conceptualize an integrated global corporation, anxiety about looking less than competent in front of peers and subordinates, unexpressed desires for themselves and the business, and cross-cultural communications (especially stereotyping related to the South American president's "emotional and looscy-goosey" style). All these issues and more were impacting the team's ability to engage the president's dream of an integrated corporation. We made the decision to focus the retreat primarily on conceptualizing an integrated company because it seemed central to the dream, and was more task-oriented and therefore less scary, than focusing on the team's relationships. The task could also be realistically completed within two days and thereby give the team a sense of accomplishment and momentum.

During the retreat the president constantly reminded the team that their purpose was to explore possibilities of organizing Comfort Foods as an integrated company. The team was encouraged to focus on moving forward in the discussion of possibilities rather than on the personal motives of any particular executive. Questioning or challenging a person's motives was discouraged by establishing a norm that anyone could say what they wanted without having to defend their point. The only requirement was to listen and to stay on topic.

Placing emphasis on listening without questioning motives, and on accomplishing the exploration task, seemed to help the executives engage more fully with each other. Occasional comments to help draw out the thinking and assumptions behind a remark and to summarize ideas and progress also helped establish a tone that everyone was sincerely contributing their best thoughts and expertise.

Throughout the two days—and, indeed, in the planning sessions leading up to the retreat—I had to "look in the mirror" more than once to avoid creating

(continues)

(continued)

psychological threats that might trigger covert behaviors in the team. Those moments were usually related to my own beliefs about what was enough safety, and what should or could be addressed by this team. I had to remind myself periodically that holding the meeting at all was a big risk for the president and for all the participants.

What I considered to be relatively mild confrontations between confident and powerful executives were in their eyes dangerous conflicts or threats to be avoided or downplayed. They were also uncomfortable with exploring interpersonal and intercultural issues, even though the impact of these on their effectiveness as a group seemed very clear to me. Those issues eventually were addressed in later retreats, after they had built greater comfort and confidence as a team that allowed exploring previously un-discussable topics.

Finally, I did my best to stay within the original expectation of exploring the possibility of an integrated organization. This they succeeded in doing, for by the end of the meeting they had unanimously agreed on the broad outlines of a global matrix structure organized by function and geography. Furthermore— partly as a way to more tightly integrate the matrix, and partly as a political move to keep a consensus—some members of the top team were "double-hatted." The executive vice president of the Americas region, for example, was also named the executive vice president of manufacturing worldwide. In fact, by the end of the retreat all the executives expressed hopeful excitement that Comfort Foods could become a globally integrated company. Perhaps all of them had secretly shared some version of the president's dream. Following the success of the retreat, they asked for help in looking at ways to increase their effectiveness as an integrated team. Having agreed on the outlines of an integrated business structure, working on their relationships was now seen by one and all as an important business task.

Conclusion

Five basic keys provide the fundamentals needed to deal effectively with covert processes in a focal system. If nothing more elaborate or complex is done, following these basic keys should increase your effectiveness in engaging covert dynamics. The most important key is the prime directive to create psychological safety. Whenever I am pretty sure there are covert issues not being expressed, I ask myself: *What is risky about this through their prism; and what can I do to make conditions safer?* Sometimes I have to accept that not all situations can be made safe enough to explore all covert processes.

CHAPTER 6

Putting Things On-the-Table

How do you go about putting something covert on-the-table for open engagement? Think about setting a table for dinner, preparing an attractive and delicious meal, creating an atmosphere conducive to conversation, and inviting folks to join in. You wouldn't order people to eat a poorly prepared, unappetizing meal for their own good! Four approaches help to ensure success when you prepare to put anything on-the-table:

1. Establish legitimacy.

2. Create enabling conditions.

3. Be strategic.

4. Be subtle, sometimes.

Let's explore each of them in some detail to learn the nuances involved in being a good host.

Establish Legitimacy

The Covert Processes Model tells us that when something is considered to be questionable, illegitimate, unacceptable, or even too good to be true, it will remain hidden, denied, or unexpressed. Conversely, anything considered legitimate, proper, acceptable, or reasonable can be put on-the-table for engagement. Thus it is clear that establishing legitimacy to address something is necessary before putting it on-the-table. Establishing legitimacy also adds to creating safety, the prime prerequisite for covert processes work, because people usually feel safe to do what is considered acceptable, proper, or appropriate.

Six aspects need attention when you are creating legitimacy. They are the "who, what, why, when, where, and how" of legitimacy. You won't be able to put something on-the-table if the focal system challenges the legitimacy or appropriateness of doing so in any of the following ways:

- **Who?** *You have no right to raise that.*

- **What?** *That is not an appropriate topic to discuss.*

- **Why?** *That is not an acceptable reason.*

- **When?** *This is not the appropriate time.*

- **Where?** *This is not the appropriate place.*

- **How?** *That is not the right way to do it.*

You must create conditions that will lead the focal system to agree it is right for *you* to raise that *topic,* for those *reasons*, in this *time* and *place*, in that *way*. If you can accomplish this, some important conditions will have been met to put things on-the-table. Next we discuss how to create legitimacy for each of the six challenges. The more legitimacy you can create, the greater the likelihood that you will be able to engage the covert issues.

Who Can Raise the Issue

Explore **who** is an appropriate or acceptable person to raise the issue in the focal system. Is it an insider, an outsider, the boss, a senior member of the group, or an expert consultant? Find out who would be considered legitimate and get that person to raise the topic. You can also create legitimacy by giving the focal system itself a mandate to explore the issue. Tell everyone, "We all need to pay attention to the ways our untested assumptions may be limiting our ability to come up with new ideas."

An outside consultant is sometimes advocated on the grounds that the consultant would be less biased—and therefore more legitimate. This can work when outsiders are actually perceived to be more expert or less biased than insiders. Sometimes, however, outsiders are challenged as not knowing enough to be helpful: *What does a consultant know about our business?*

Some focal systems may insist it would be difficult or even impossible to find anyone who could be viewed as legitimate to raise certain covert issues. At such times, you may need to challenge limiting beliefs in the focal system's prism: *Why are we questioning the finance officer's right to ask about our budget difficulties?* Chapters 7 and 8 discuss ways to challenge and modify limiting beliefs in a focal system's prism. It is also possible that the threat level is still too high to proceed. If so, you need to create a greater sense of safety.

What Can Be Addressed

What you want the focal system to address also needs to be viewed as legitimate before you put it on-the-table. Sometimes appeals to precedents or to future needs can be effective: *Remember, we looked at our unspoken assumptions when we reorganized in 1998. Because of changing conditions, we need to reexamine all our assumptions, otherwise we'll just repeat the past.*

It helps to list the topic as part of the official agenda or as an official purpose of the meeting. People are more likely to discuss "forbidden" topics when they are officially sanctioned to do so; this feels safer than dealing with something that comes up informally. You can also link the topic you wish to put on-the-table to an issue or project that is widely perceived as important and legitimate: *This is related to whether we'll be successful with the project proposed by the CEO.* This technique is more effective than hoping the topic's importance and legitimacy is self-evident. If it were really self-evident, wouldn't it have already been addressed?

Why It Needs to Be Addressed

Be ready to present good reasons **why** it's important to address a covert issue. Remember that the reasons must be seen as legitimate by the focal system through its prism. An emotional appeal may fall on deaf ears if the prism says: *Don't be swayed by emotions, listen to logic.* On the other hand, you can harness the beliefs in the prism of the focal system to justify exploring the covert dynamic. If the focal system has a belief that it is all right to address any topic that would increase profitability, then you may need to show how addressing your topic could lead to increased profitability. If you cannot do this, then the blocking beliefs in the focal system's prism will have to be confronted.

When to Address the Issue

You may also need to establish **when** is an appropriate time to put the topic or issue on-the-table. Is it at a special three-day planning session? When the organization is riding a wave of success? In the pits of failure? Before the new boss is hired? After the new boss is hired? You are trying to establish some answer other than "not now," "later," or "never."

You need to find a time that the focal system considers acceptable to put the issue on-the-table: *All right, we won't address that now, but I'll put it on the agenda for our upcoming staff retreat.* If that is impractical because the appropriate time won't occur for years *(When we get a new CEO is the time to do that)*, try to negotiate: *Yes, I know it's usually best to wait until we get a new CEO, but conditions have changed . . .* or *the new CEO has signaled the need for a fresh start . . .* or *this isn't like the other things, this can't wait!* Whatever approach you take, it must respect, or explicitly confront, the focal system's beliefs about legitimate timing.

Where Is the Right Place

You need to establish **where** there is a legitimate place to engage your issue. The weekly staff meeting might not be considered appropriate, but a special off-site retreat called for that purpose could be. Once again you are trying to establish an answer other than "not here," "not there," "no where." If there is a setting (e.g., a training room vs. the supervisor's office) that is considered more appropriate than others, try to meet there. To put something covert on-the-table, you must consider the focal system's beliefs about legitimate locations.

How Can the Issue Be Addressed

Establishing legitimacy for **how** something will be addressed often requires you to do one or more of the following:

- Remind people whenever possible that the proposed method was used successfully in the past. For example, a work group may have cleaned up some messy team issues during a team development session two years ago.

- Explain how the method has been used by a respected individual, group, or organization. For example: *Remember the CEO called a special meeting to deal with this sort of thing last year. This is Pat Smith, the president of Covert Enterprises, who is here to tell us how they got their breakthrough. Here's a journal article that describes the method and how it was used successfully in four companies like ours.*

- Remind people that the proposed method is known to be associated with addressing the kind of issues you wish to put on-the-table. For example: *Everyone here knows you do team building if you want to address those kinds of things. We've always said we need to work in different ways in order to be more creative.*

If all approaches are met with some variant of *That's not the right way to do it* or *That won't work here*, then confronting the blocking beliefs in the focal system's prism may need to be your next step.

Focal systems differ considerably in their beliefs about legitimacy in addressing covert issues. Some ways of creating legitimacy, however, are more likely to succeed than others. Compare the following vignettes:

- Consider a scenario with an HR manager announcing there is a need to look at blind spots because people aren't really thinking about what they're doing. A half-day session in the plant will be facilitated by a real guru who will help people understand how they think, using right-brain techniques.

- Now consider this scenario. The CEO says it's important to look at organizational blind spots because they are impacting our productivity and market share. This is based on interviews conducted by a representative task force chaired by the VP of manufacturing. We will engage in a special four-day retreat with follow-up sessions at a conference center to address these concerns. The retreat will be facilitated by a well-known expert who has worked on blind spots with other companies in our industry.

There is a good chance this session will actually happen and that it might achieve some noticeable results.

Create Enabling Conditions

Once you have established enough legitimacy to place an issue on-the-table, you need to create the conditions that allow it to be addressed. Otherwise, it will just get knocked off-the-table, or be worked around. There are several things you can do.

Clear the Table

Sometimes issues remain covert because there is no room to put anything else on-the-table. The focal system's plate is full. Only so much can be addressed at any given time: *We don't have time to look at that, we have customers to meet and reports to write and reviews to give and. . . .* It has become commonplace to maintain such "full plates" that it becomes impossible to address difficult or uncomfortable issues. This is itself a covert process (avoidance, denial, collusion). Also familiar is that, just when a difficult topic is about to be addressed, additional items mysteriously appear and each is more pressing than the item being avoided.

You then need to clear the table and keep it clear long enough to allow the covert issue to be put on-the-table and addressed; it can be more important to help take things off people's plates than to add one more thing. Establishing the reason that addressing the covert issue is a priority topic is one way to do this. It is a clue that some kind of covert process is at work when people claim to have too much on their plates and cannot imagine how to take anything off.

Invite Rather Than Order

Actions to draw attention to a covert issue are best formulated as invitations rather than orders. This is not an issue of politeness. An invitation implies that people have choice, as well as control over how much, how quickly, and how far to go. Remember that these are key ingredients for creating and maintaining a sense of safety. Asking a group if they would be interested in looking at some aspect of their behavior through a different lens is different from telling them they won't get anywhere until they deal with their emotions (*So who'll be first to share what they're* really *feeling?*). Finally, create a climate of inquiry and curiosity, rather than blame or fault finding. This establishes a more inviting atmosphere for exploring possible covert dynamics.

Frame the Issue

The way something is framed determines how people will react to it. The focal system is unlikely to go on a fishing expedition, but they might readily search for "additional clues to a puzzle." If a group's favorite theme is *We're a really good group*, asking them to look at unexpressed negative feelings about each other may go nowhere. However, pointing out that a characteristic of most good groups is the ability to share a full range of feelings may pique their curiosity.

To frame issues in enabling ways, you need a good sense of the focal system's prism. Your presentation of the issue must be seen as enabling through the prism of the focal system with whom you are working. Suggesting that individuals confront the boss at the upcoming retreat "because it will be a safe setting" may be viewed negatively if some people got into trouble when they were too candid at an office party. Creating a setting where the boss reveals some areas for self-improvement and then sincerely asks for feedback could be more enabling. Always keep in mind that our cultural prisms have an impact on how things are viewed. Confronting the boss may be perceived differently depending on where in the world you do it.

Identify Motivation

Few people willingly enter into a scary situation unless they believe it is ultimately in their own best interest, or they are motivated to do so for other reasons. You must create enough motivation or self-interest for the focal system to look under-the-table. "Trust me, this is for your own good!" is rarely sufficient. Highlighting the potential benefits of engaging a covert issue will help overcome the fear associated with looking under-the-table.

When you help people become more aware of the impact of out-of-awareness patterns you may develop motivation for further exploration. For example, telling a co-worker who asks how a presentation went with the boss: *You lower your voice when talking to the boss, and the boss pays more attention to people who speak louder.* This might spark motivation for the person to learn more about their pattern.

Avoid Accusations

Avoid attributing evil motivations to the focal system's behavior; it will be easier to address the behavior if there are no negative judgments about its source. Accusatory inquiries are generally perceived as a threat and lead to even greater protection of whatever is being hidden. Even if the focal system's motivations and behavior are inappropriate or self-serving, it is unlikely that a blaming approach will lead to anything except denials.

Conversely, you are more likely to create a setting conducive to exploring covert processes when you are curious, assume the focal system is trying the best it can, and remember that whatever is hidden may be out of the focal system's awareness, or being hidden out of fear.

Thus, few people will admit to being a "self-serving liar," but most might allow that they "misspoke," or "didn't have all the facts," or, better still, "spoke only from one point of view." Allowing that people are usually trying the best they can helps stimulate disclosure and exploration rather than defensiveness. Never corner anyone. Always allow people to save face.

Creating enough legitimacy to put something on-the-table is not enough. You need to create the climate and conditions that encourage people to successfully engage the covert issue.

Be Strategic

Multiple covert processes are present in any situation. Only a limited number can be engaged at any given time, so try to be strategic in choosing what to focus on. The following are some considerations to keep in mind.

Assess Readiness

Issues may be more or less potent at a particular time. People may not be ready to address something because the timing is inappropriate, they are not motivated enough, or they are too afraid. At another time, the same issues may be ready to be engaged, perhaps because they have been simmering for awhile. Whatever the reasons, attempting to work a covert process before the focal system is ready leads nowhere. When everything is going well it may be impossible to address excessive competition between product divisions. But, raising it after a very difficult year, when leaders are saying *Everyone is not on the same page* might be more successful.

Attend to Sequencing

Sometimes the order in which things are addressed can make a difference. The focal system may finally be ready to put its pie-in-the-sky dreams on-the-table, but first it needs to address a limiting belief in its prism that dreaming is a waste of time. Sometimes it's appropriate to address one issue simply because it helps prepare the focal system to work on a more difficult one. Challenging the less important beliefs in the focal system's prism can establish a comfortable mode of operation before going on to the more important ones. For example, challenging beliefs about staff functions may open the door for later challenges to a specific line operation.

Evaluate Centrality

Depending on what the focal system is trying to accomplish, some covert processes are more central than others. In certain situations it may be important for people to express their negative feelings, but more central to address the absence of hopes and dreams that fuel those feelings. Or, there may be a core belief within the prism that, unless addressed, will block certain possibilities: *We shouldn't waste our time dreaming, we have real work to do.*

Some topics, some things, and some people are more central than others. Addressing a hidden dynamic involving the team leader has a different impact than addressing that of another member of the group. Addressing a limiting belief about how the core work of the business gets done may be more powerful than addressing how supplies are distributed. Talking about visions, hopes, and dreams for a more open workplace has a different impact than expressing hopes for a more efficiently run Monday morning staff meeting.

Assess Your Role and Responsibilities

At times you may need to renegotiate expectations about your role and responsibilities in order to address previously unforeseen issues. You may have agreed to work with a group on their interpersonal relationships, but their patterns of behavior start to suggest fundamental issues of racism or sexism that transcend interpersonal dynamics. If that hunch begins to dominate your focus, it is clear that you will need to renegotiate expectations in order to proceed. On the other hand, you may note that team members rarely express any hopes or dreams, but choose not to pursue that because it is not central to the immediate task.

Look in the Mirror

This is a reminder to address covert issues when you believe you have the necessary skills, knowledge, and experience to be helpful. You need to look in the mirror and know your strengths and limits in dealing with different types of covert processes. You should also refrain from acting (or refer the situation to someone more qualified) rather than identifying covert issues that you lack the skill to handle.

Because multiple covert processes are always at work, thinking strategically about which to address, and when, will help guide your actions and ensure a greater chance of success.

Be Subtle Sometimes

Sometimes it is not possible to speak directly to, or about, a covert issue in a focal system. Nonetheless, it is still possible to address covert issues if you are willing to operate with subtlety. Using subtlety can achieve impressive results, but remember that it is unlikely to be noticed and won't generate credit or applause. If you are willing to be gratified more by movement than acknowledgment, here are some subtle ways to consider addressing covert processes without explicitly naming them.

Do Only What Is Needed

When a covert dynamic is driven by fear or is out-of-awareness, publicly calling attention to it may only lead to adamant denials and deeper resistance. On the other hand, just doing what is needed, without comment, may achieve movement. It could also lay the groundwork for more explicit engagement of the covert dynamic at a later time. Suppose, based on your knowledge and experience, you see a covert dynamic at work and just do something helpful, without comment. No time-outs, no processing, no fanfare, no learning moment. Just do what you think would be helpful.

By being subtle, you may let the opportunity pass to address and resolve the covert issue. It also fails to provide an opportunity for the focal system to learn for the future. However, not all covert issues can be addressed all the time, in all settings—nor do they all need to be addressed. Ask yourself the question: *Is it critical to put this covert dynamic on-the-table, or is it more appropriate to encourage movement in the moment?*

Instead of trying to get unspoken leadership issues about the absence of direction on-the–table, you suggest setting an agenda and purpose for the meeting. Instead of pointing out that the group needs to address its unspoken norm of negativity, you suggest people say what they like about something as well as what they don't like. Instead of putting the absence of emotion on-the-table, you describe your own emotions. None of these actions will permanently fix the system because they don't directly address the limiting covert dynamic. Each does have a chance of achieving movement, and that may be all that is possible for the moment.

Address the Issue Indirectly

Even though some covert processes may not be available for open discussion doesn't mean they can't be addressed. It only means you have to address them indirectly and that you are unlikely to get a direct reply. How do you address a covert issue indirectly? The following are some ways to consider:

- **Give a presentation or tell a story.** Find a reason to give a presentation or tell a story that addresses the suspected covert issue. If there are unspoken leadership issues in a team, tell a story about team leadership that includes the suspected dynamics, without saying: *And now here's a presentation that speaks to your problem!* If people later ask *Hey, how does that apply to us?* encourage them to discuss it. If they go ahead and change their behavior without comment, let them do that too.

  Schein (1999), in reporting on a presentation to an executive team, commented that "Although the overt purpose of this educational intervention was to present some formal material to the executives, a covert purpose was to involve them in thinking more realistically about their own culture and its consequences" (p. 23).

- **Model behavior.** You can always model unblocked behavior without calling attention to it as a demonstration of desired behavior. Simply model by your own actions what needs to be on-the-table. If the focal system is afraid of something, you can be fearless. If people seem blind to possibilities, demonstrate vision. If people act foolhardy, you can be cautious. If others are defensive, you can be vulnerable. If they are stuck, you can move. Remember, actions always speak louder than words, especially when dealing with covert processes.

- **Communicate using the 4 M's.** The use of symbolic means of communication is another subtle way to address covert issues. Changing physical arrangements or seating patterns can be a way to speak indirectly to certain issues. For example, if by their physical arrangement people are confronting one another, lined up for or against something, or simply separated, then physically rearranging them could change the dynamics.

  The use of music, media, and metaphors can also be employed to send a subtle message about the covert issue. Noting the rhythm or tempo of a focal group can be an effective way to say: *Things are dragging,* or *People are rushing out-of-control,* or *People are out-of-sync, they are not listening to each other.* Drawing a visual image of the focal system or painting a word picture are other ways to communicate indirectly. An offhand observation that the focal system is behaving like a bunch of kids at recess, or a plane with one engine out, may have more impact than a more direct comment that can be blocked or defended.

  Our conscious, literal minds are often well-defended against information we do not wish to know, but the same information delivered symbolically can be understood by our unconscious. A symbolic message might be understood, and acted on, while a direct statement could elicit nothing more than strong denials.

- **Use rituals and symbols.** Rituals and symbols are another way to deal indirectly with covert factors that are blocking movement.

A focal system with an unacknowledged fear that things might get out of control if allowed to continue is likely to shut itself down for fear of consequences. Increasing the rituals and symbols associated with being in control could ease the fear without needing to address it directly. It may seem unnecessary to take the time explicitly to remind people of the norms, of established processes, of who's "in charge," and of how difficult issues will be handled. However, on a symbolic level they are all reminders that there are provisions for order and safety, and that can be quietly reassuring.

Doing things in established ways, almost ritualistically, can be a symbolic reminder of familiarity and constancy and help with unspoken fears about the uncertainties that lie ahead. Evoking powerful images in the focal system's culture, such as a beloved founder or famous organizational story, are also ways of introducing themes to address covert issues without speeches and fanfare. For example, retelling stories about the successful handling of the crisis back in 1985 is a subtle way to challenge unspoken beliefs that *There is nothing we can do. The situation is outside of our control.*

Sometimes directly addressing covert processes is just not possible, for whatever reasons. When that happens more subtle approaches may still achieve desired movement. The following case highlights the four approaches for putting things on-the-table during a critical moment at the beginning of a major change project.

U.S. Department of Agriculture

The Case of the Common Program Structure

As a science policy analyst in the U.S. Department of Agriculture, I was put in charge of an intergovernmental task force to study the feasibility of creating a "common program structure" to classify all agricultural research. The U.S. Government funds hundreds of federal agricultural research facilities and also distributes grants to state agricultural experiment stations in all the states. The competition for allocation of funds is always fierce, and especially so between the states and the feds. Although in some ways they were both *competitors* for funds and *collaborators* in research, the two sides always referred to each other publicly as "our collaborators."

The only inventory of publicly funded agricultural research was the Current Research Inventory System (CRIS), which documented a specific research project's scope, methodology, and progress. Aggregates of CRIS information could be compiled, but different organizations used different taxonomies, making it difficult or impossible to see the whole picture. There was intense pressure from the funding committees of Congress to account for the whole picture and do strategic planning across all the agricultural research entities. This was not possible without baseline data, and the taskforce was created to explore ways to develop baselines for planning purposes.

The task force was composed of nine members representing the interests of the major collaborators, and I was the only person without an agricultural science background. Part of my job was to achieve a collaborative outcome despite the hidden competitive pressures that had disrupted previous joint task force efforts.

The Paper Napkin Caper

The task force met for a three-day planning session at a research facility near Peoria, Illinois. The first day was filled with challenges: *This is silly, it's not possible to develop a common program structure. We can't tamper with the CRIS structure. Why are we doing this? What use will it have for research?* I wondered if these comments were covert ways to block progress on a task each side feared might advantage the other in fund allocations. These competitive pressures could not be openly discussed because we were meeting as "collaborators." Though I explained repeatedly that our purpose was to develop a way to assist planning, not tamper with funding, the topic of a common program structure kept getting knocked off-the-table.

Frustrated by the inability to get any movement, I came up with an idea that might bypass the blocking comments and put the feasibility of a common program structure on-the-table. When we broke for dinner I asked everyone

(continues)

(continued)

to write on a paper napkin how they would lump all agricultural research into no more than five to seven "pots." When everyone returned to the meeting room they saw flip charts hanging on the walls with the napkins taped to them. It took no more than a moment for everyone to see that the categorizations were essentially the same: animal science, plant science, soil and water science, post-harvest technologies, and, on some, human nutrition. There were differences in wordings, such as livestock and veterinary sciences instead of animal science, that had important meanings for the participants, but the commonality of all responses was inescapable.

After expressing amazement at my "magic trick," they began to talk about how such a categorization could be useful. I pointed out that no such summaries existed, and that it could be helpful in seeking funding and aligning support from different constituencies. The CRIS structure would not need to be modified—only the ways data were aggregated at high levels. For the first time they seemed to understand we were developing something for policy and budgetary planning, not intruding on science experiments. For my part, I believed if we could reach consensus even at the level of five to seven categories it would be valuable, and over time more detailed categorizations would emerge because policymakers would demand the information. For the rest of our work together, the feasibility of a common program structure was squarely on-the-table of the task force.

The Four Approaches in Action

A quick review of the four approaches reveals that most were involved in getting the common program structure on-the-table of the task force. This was a situation where I intentionally sought to achieve movement and did not confront members about their unspoken competitive dynamics. Legitimacy had already been created by having a joint federal-state science committee mandate the task force and then ensuring that all involved parties were represented. I was considered relatively neutral—not aligned with one scientific discipline over another. Holding a multi-day planning session was recognized as the proper way to do things. Also important, the meeting was held at a research facility in the agricultural heartland, not in Washington, D.C. Convening a three-day offsite meeting also allowed the participants to concentrate on the task at hand. Furthermore, there was pressure from important funding sources to focus on the project and be prepared to report back to them, and this created additional legitimacy and urgency.

The napkin activity combined multiple approaches in one simple intervention. First, it was playful and could be interpreted as an invitation to see what would happen rather than an order to develop options. It enabled framing the feasibility of developing a classification structure, which had been questioned throughout the day. It also quickly revealed the commonalities in the room, thereby reducing concerns about the difficulties of reaching consensus across multiple actors and constituencies.

Once people saw that a common structure was possible at a high level, and that it did not directly threaten their separate interests, they could begin to see how it might *advance* their mutual interest to increase funding. Any unexpressed doubts about spending time on the task force, or whether the "collaborators" could or should reach consensus, could be dispelled without directly challenging anyone's motives or intentions. Asking the task force through the napkin activity to develop agreement on five to seven major categories was done with strategic intent. It was feasible, clearly central to everything, consistent with my role as task force chair, and easy to do. The task force members may actually have been ready to engage the topic, despite appearances to the contrary. Finally, the strategy of asking a bunch of scientists to write something on the back of a dinner napkin probably falls into the category of being subtle.

Conclusion

Recognizing that a covert dynamic may be at work is one thing. Being able to put the covert topic on-the-table in ways that it can be engaged is still another. In many cases, however, that is all you will need to do. The focal system will often be capable of addressing a previously hidden topic or issue once it has been identified and legitimately placed on-the-table in enabling ways.

CHAPTER 7

► # Recognizing and Rethinking Interventions

According to the Covert Processes Model, every focal system has a prism of beliefs that interprets and makes meaning of the world. Those things the prism interprets as being "legitimate, proper, acceptable, or reasonable" can be put on-the-table and engaged; anything interpreted through the prism as "unacceptable or illegitimate" is denied or unexpressed. Sometimes you need to confront one or more blocking beliefs in the focal system's prism in order to put something on-the-table and engage it successfully. How do we confront beliefs in the prism of a focal system?

Interventions and the Prism

Three types of interventions can be chosen to confront beliefs in a focal system's prism. They are actions that help the focal system recognize, rethink, or reframe one or more of the tacit beliefs in its prism:

- **Recognizing interventions** involve anything that helps the focal system realize how out-of-awareness beliefs located in its prism may be blocking it from seeing or dealing with important issues. As an example, front-line workers may be blocked from taking innovative actions in response to new conditions or unexpected difficulties by tacit beliefs about ensuring "safety" and avoidance of risk.

- **Rethinking interventions** involve ways to encourage the focal system to reconsider previously untested assumptions and beliefs. This usually follows recognition by the focal system that its current beliefs are limiting its desired performance or potential. Blind spots and blocks in the prism can be addressed by contrasting limiting beliefs with new possibilities. For example, IBM's turnaround in recent years involved rethinking core assumptions about mainframe computers, services, and solutions.

- **Reframing interventions** change the way something is experienced by altering the way it is framed by the prism. Note that changing the framing doesn't imply changing the reality; rather, reframing alters the meaning and interpretation that the focal system makes about a "fact," thereby changing the way the system sees itself and its possibilities. Whether the glass is half-full or half-empty depends on how you frame it. Reframing the way something is experienced allows for new possibilities and options. There is a difference between *We can't do it* and *We haven't figured it out yet.*

These three types of interventions can be pursued separately or in combination. Moving from recognition to rethinking or reframing is a natural progression. The remainder of this chapter addresses recognizing and rethinking interventions. Reframing interventions are the topic of Chapter 8.

Recognizing Interventions

Recognizing interventions are actions or activities designed to help the focal system recognize how previously unaddressed or untested beliefs are preventing important issues from being put on-the-table. In many cases this is all that is needed to enable the normal problem-solving processes of the focal system to address and resolve the issue(s).

An Organizational Example

One example of a recognition intervention is to use the Covert Processes Model as a diagnostic framework for organizational inquiry by a top team, task force, or corporate work group. This could be effective if the focal system is interested in looking at its own dynamics as part of an improvement effort or at hidden factors that may be blocking a change initiative. The well-known imagery of on-the-table or under-the-table can be used by the group itself, or it can be used with the help of a consultant. Usually unconscious dimensions are not included in this kind of exercise.

The first step is to clarify the purpose of the exercise and set appropriate ground rules designed to establish legitimacy and safety. Then members of the focal system, individually or in subgroups, complete several diagnostic statements. A slightly modified version of the Covert Processes Group Diagnostic Worksheet introduced in Chapter 3 could also be used for this purpose:

- **What's on-the-table?** The acceptable, legitimate, or proper behaviors, feelings, and issues that we openly talk about and address in this organization are . . .

- **What's under-the-table?** The unacceptable, illegitimate, or questionable behaviors, feelings, and issues that we avoid and deny in this organization are . . .

- **What's above-the-clouds?** The secret hopes, wishes, or aspirations that we don't speak about in this organization are . . .

- **What's in the prism?** The core beliefs, values, or assumptions that help create and maintain the way things are in this organization are . . .

- **What's in the subconscious?** (optional, depending on willingness and skills to consider unconscious dynamics) The buried or repressed behaviors, feelings, and issues we ignore in this organization are . . .

- **What's in the superconscious?** (optional, depending on willingness and skills to consider unconscious dynamics) The untapped creativity, potential, or capabilities of this organization and its people are . . .

Responses, recorded on flip charts displayed on the walls, show what people currently believe is on-the-table, under-the-table, above-the-clouds, in the prism, and, possibly, in the unconscious of the focal organization. Often such a visual display provides a powerful and tangible picture of the reasons things are the way they are and what needs to be addressed in order for things to be different. The visual display also helps people see the dynamics and interrelationships among the different elements (e.g., why certain beliefs in the prism keep important discussions from happening).

Assuming no other covert blocking factors are present, the members of the focal organization then discuss actions to address whatever has been recognized as needing attention. This kind of diagnostic session can be done in a one- to two-day retreat, depending on the participants' experience with self-reflection, organizational diagnosis, and team-building. In a major division of one organization, this type of diagnostic inquiry led a management team to provide the responses summarized below. In this instance, it was not part of the exercise to look at what might be in the unconscious.

Responses to Diagnostic Questions

What we openly talk about (on-the-table):

- End results
- The bottom line
- Stock prices
- Being nice
- Logical, rational thinking
- Eating lunch together
- Our families and vacations

- How controlled we are by "them"
- Structural changes
- The need for loyalty

What we avoid or deny in our discussions (under-the-table):

- Any expression of feelings, especially sadness and crying
- Competition for power and success
- Being allowed to be an individual
- Why executive salaries and perks are so high when business isn't going well
- The need for layoffs
- Conflicting positions or opinions
- Why there aren't more women VPs
- Our fears about the business and our future
- Questions of competence

What we don't discuss because it's too good to be true (above-the-clouds):

- People who support other people would be recognized and rewarded
- People would talk *to*, not about, each other
- We can make a difference
- We would practice what we preach
- We would adopt new-paradigm thinking
- Teams and teamwork would flourish
- Our vision would be so clear and powerful that people would jump on-board

- We could achieve a breakthrough that would lead to greater success and stability

- Everyone would be treated with dignity and respect

Implicit core beliefs, values, and assumptions that keep us the way we are (in the prism):

- Showing emotions is a sign of weakness (Men don't cry)

- There's nothing we can do until the people upstairs take action

- It's a dog-eat-dog world

- People should conform and fit in; no one likes a troublemaker

- Laying people off is an admission of failure

- The only thing that counts in business is the bottom line

- We're not good at thinking outside the box

- Keep doing what made us successful in the past

- Business is a man's world

- It's not safe to tell the truth

Based on these responses, visually displayed on a wall, the management team quickly recognized why things were the way they were and why they were stuck. For example, they saw the beliefs in their prism that "business is a man's world" and recognized the absence of women VPs. They also realized that, to put some things on-the-table for discussion and action, such as addressing "our fears about the business and our future," would require a combination of steps:

1. **Taking some things off-the-table** to create more time, space and energy. For example, stop talking about "our families and vacations."

2. **Activating unspoken hopes,** for example, talking more about how "we could achieve a breakthrough that would lead to greater success and stability."

3. **Challenging some limiting beliefs** contained within their prism. For example, rethink the unspoken belief that they should "keep doing what made us successful in the past."

Seeing these interrelationships gave them renewed energy and provided hope that they could, in fact, do something that would make a difference in their organization. This led to more focused and somewhat emotional discussions of what needed to be done to turn things around. Whether or not the actions decided upon would lead to future success, the management team felt they had finally **recognized** some of the factors, patterns, and limiting beliefs that were covertly holding them back.

A Work Group Example

Another example is provided by a work group that recognized a pattern in their behaviors was linked to their prism and was having unintended and undesirable consequences. People in the InfoTech Division (ITD) prided themselves on their intelligence, analytic skills, rationality, and ability to find the objectively "right" answer to any problem. Nonetheless, the manager of ITD asked an internal human resources consultant to help with a general concern that there was too much "politics" going on in the division.

When asked by the HR consultant to define *politics,* the response was "You know, getting together to work out 'deals' in advance before we discuss things as a group; that sort of thing." The HR consultant asked permission to observe a few ITD meetings and conduct some limited interviews to get a sense of the situation. Not too long after, at a special divisional retreat, the HR consultant described the following dynamics, based on the interviews and observations (comments in quotes are from the interview data):

1. Getting the "right answer" seems terribly important to everyone. Any possible error or omission is "ruthlessly" attacked by other members of the group. Any presentation in the group has to be able to withstand close scrutiny and emerge "fault- or error-free." "No error or omission or typo is too small to escape notice."

2. People dislike making presentations "because of the hostile environment," but no one is willing to say anything because it would be "judged as a sign of weakness or a willingness to tolerate mistakes."

3. Any potential conflicts or arguments over data at divisional meetings are quickly ended with disapproving comments to either "do your homework in advance" or "don't get too emotional."

4. Consequently, people liked to be able to prepare "bullet-proof" presentations in advance that could "withstand any attack."

After presenting these observations, along with other data from the interviews, the consultant asked those assembled if the pattern seemed accurate. Almost everyone smiled, saying *Yes, you hit the nail on the head,* or *You did a good job of describing the way it is around here.* When asked why people behaved that way: *We have no choice. Because of what we do we can't afford to make any mistakes. We've got to get it right the first time.*

The HR consultant then asked what impact their assumption about "having to have the right answer" might have on politics at ITD. At first everyone seemed confused by the question, but with a little prodding they realized what the HR consultant was getting at. Because being attacked for not having the right answer was so unpleasant, people who had "been around" got together in advance to make sure there were no problems with their presentations. Thus, relatively little was really discussed in the meetings during their presentations, because everything had been worked out in advance.

Meetings became a series of choreographed presentations where people nit-picked or attacked the presentations that had not been worked out in advance. Recognizing this pattern and wanting to have more open discussions, the manager and ITD team formulated a problem statement: "How do we ensure quality discussions and decisions as a group and also ensure that we catch mistakes and deliver the right answer?" Eventually, they decided they needed to do two things:

1. Ensure what left the division had no mistakes, but seek thorough discussions and different points of view within the division.

2. Reduce or change the hostile environment of divisional meetings to encourage more openness and sharing.

Once the Info Tech Division **recognized** that an acknowledged pattern of behavior might be having undesirable consequences, they were in a position to apply their own problem-solving skills. It helped that they were able to see both the functional and dysfunctional aspects of their beliefs and pattern. This allowed them to seek solutions that addressed their concerns about errors and mistakes as well to improve the quality of their interactions.

An Individual Example

The next example is about a manager who recognized a self-defeating behavior pattern based on outdated lessons learned from childhood. Chris, the new manager of a work group, was beginning to get a reputation for "rude," "bullying," and "controlling" behavior in staff meetings. Many saw it as power going to the head of an immature new manager. In any event, the manager's previously sterling reputation was now becoming tarnished. Seeking out a former mentor in the organization, Chris confessed that "Something did happen at staff meetings, but not what people think." The manager went on to say: "Frankly, I'm not sure what happens. I just have a need, almost a compulsion, to get 'my air time.' It's really silly. After all, I am the boss."

The mentor suggested that the manager track and record whenever this "compulsion" occurred and report back. Some weeks later Chris met again with the mentor and reported that the "compulsion" seemed to happen only during staff meetings. Both were puzzled, but they decided to have lunch before thinking about what to do next. At lunch they sat with a few other colleagues, the manager happening to sit at the head of the table. During lunch Chris began to interrupt others and push to get ideas out. The mentor saw what was happening and quietly pointed out the behavior pattern. Later Chris explained an insight that had been revealed at that moment:

> I come from a large family. Growing up, when we sat around the table to eat either my mother or father told us kids to keep quiet while they talked. They were not reluctant to tell us to be quiet, talk over us, interrupt us, whatever, so they could talk. I hadn't thought of it before, but when I sit in staff meetings, at the head of the table, it's as if I have the right to talk and no one else matters. I'm really embarrassed.

Whether or not this was the real reason for the behavior pattern, Chris vowed never to sit at the head of the table unless giving a speech. After four months or so, the mentor was pleased to hear through the grapevine that Chris was a "new person" and any potential problems had been straightened out.

In this episode, the problematic behavior may have been rooted in old family history, the data collection haphazard, and the moment of insight serendipitous, but **recognition** of the pattern led to successful remedial action. Of course, the moment of insight would never have occurred if neither the manager nor the mentor felt it was safe and legitimate to look for a behavior pattern.

The preceding examples illustrate that one major type of intervention related to covert processes involves bringing into awareness previously untested or unacknowledged prism beliefs that are impacting performance. Once recognized, the focal system is often capable of changing behavior without much further assistance. In other cases, however, more than recognition alone is needed, and the focal system may need to rethink or reframe its beliefs in order to encourage desired behaviors and performance.

Rethinking Interventions

Rethinking interventions involve a focal system confronting existing beliefs in its prism in order to allow new possibilities to be placed on-the-table. The first step in rethinking is almost always triggered by recognition of an unsatisfactory current pattern of thought or behavior and a desire to change it. This is followed by some form of re-evaluation of the current beliefs that are limiting performance so that new possibilities can emerge. Two forms of rethinking interventions are particularly relevant when confronting unsatisfactory beliefs and resulting behavior patterns. They are (1) double-loop learning, and (2) challenging outdated or dysfunctional beliefs that are leading to the unwanted outcomes.

Double-Loop Learning

Double-loop learning is a term used to connote a focal system's ability to examine and then modify existing beliefs and assumptions that are guiding thinking and problem-solving. In short, it is the ability to reflect upon the usually out-of-awareness mental "programming" that guides our day-to-day actions. This is different from single-loop learning, where the focal system learns how to adapt and problem-solve consistent with the untested beliefs and assumptions in its prism. The ability to address not only problems but also the logic that guides problem-solving is what makes it a double-loop process.

Usually the prism beliefs and assumptions that guide problem-solving are taken for granted and therefore hidden from consideration. Because the same beliefs and logic applied to the same situation will produce the same results (single-loop), it is only when the existing beliefs and logic are questioned (double-loop) that new possibilities emerge. Double-loop learning is a form of rethinking aimed at the focal system's prism. Chris Argyris and Donald Schön (1974) have written extensively about the concept of double-loop learning and the defensive routines that emerge to protect core beliefs and self-image. More references to their work can be found in the bibliography at the end of this book.

An example of double-loop learning occurred when a team of relatively new management negotiators achieved success in a union-management bargaining meeting after they reflected on, and challenged, some of their previously covert assumptions. These managers had approached their meeting based on a set of unexamined beliefs that included:

1. Unions can't be trusted and are always manipulating things to get what they want.

2. It's important to get on with the task and not waste time with "niceties."

3. It's a sign of trust to put your best offer on-the-table right away.

With these unexamined beliefs in their prism, the managers became convinced the union negotiators were playing games because they wanted to spend time building relationships (a "nicety") and wanted to address things one issue at a time (not putting their best offer on-the-table right away). Furthermore, these actions served to "prove" the managers were right to believe unions couldn't be trusted and would manipulate things to get what they wanted.

Before negotiations broke down completely, a break was called by the consultant working with the union-management team. During the break, the consultant asked each side to list the four to six major assumptions that were guiding how they approached negotiating, especially regarding trust, and to then share their lists. The breakthrough occurred after the managers rethought their previously unacknowledged operating assumptions because they saw the following two items on the union team's list:

1. The first thing you should do is build relationships in order to build trust. Then you can go on with the task.

2. The best way to build trust is to successfully negotiate a series of small(er) issues. Don't try to take on too much too soon.

Had the managers persisted with their original approach, without rethinking the assumptions guiding their actions (single-loop learning), it's likely the negotiations would have broken down. Instead, by challenging some of the unexamined assumptions that were guiding their view of the situation (double-loop learning), the managers were able to change their behaviors towards the union team. This allowed things to be put on-the-table that had previously been "held back" or hidden.

Challenging Outdated or Dysfunctional Beliefs

Contained within the prism that helps define reality and response for a focal system are a number of components. These were briefly introduced in Chapter 2. The components include: childhood lessons learned; beliefs, assumptions and values; formal theories and systems of thought; paradigms; and organizational and societal cultures. In many cases these contents provide useful, if not essential, perspectives for succeeding in the world. In other cases, contents that once were helpful may no longer be so, and could in fact be covertly blocking effective behavior. Absent rethinking and left unchallenged, these no longer relevant contents could prove dysfunctional to the focal system. Consider the following examples.

- **Childhood lessons learned.** A good example was mentioned earlier. As a child, were you taught "first look left, then right" before crossing the street? As an adult, do you still automatically look left then right? If you live in North America this is still a helpful childhood lesson, but if you are sent on a business trip to London, Tokyo, or Singapore, this automatic behavior will prove dangerous because cars are driven on the opposite side of the road. You could get blindsided because of an unexamined, and therefore hidden, lesson learned. Fortunately, when you are driving there are strong signals and secondary measures (placement of signs, lights) to cue you to override your habitual response. In an organizational context, such cues may be absent and people may unknowingly walk into "oncoming traffic" in a business meeting due to habitual thinking. For example, lessons learned in childhood about always deferring to others may impede your ability to take charge.

- **Beliefs, assumptions, and values.** The economic changes since the 1970s have shown more than one family the problems of (covertly) basing today's financial decisions on old values and beliefs. Many people who lived through the Great Depression of the 1930s, or were raised by those who did, learned strong values about money—especially about the evils of debt, the risks of stocks, and the merits of saving safely. During the 1950s and 1960s, when inflation was low, behaviors associated with these values served people well, which reinforced the validity of the values.

However, in the 1970s and 1980s, when inflation rates reached double-digit proportions, some people continued to save. This occurred despite the fact that bank interest rates were lower than the inflation rate, and people were actually losing money by not buying things, such as houses, that would appreciate. Mortgage debt, after all, was discounted every year as the inflation rate spiraled upward. In some cases, people eventually realized what was happening, confronted their values, and decided it was better to take on debt, but they were too late. The economic situation had changed faster than their values. Behaviors based on the assumptions of inflation proved disastrous in the recessionary economy of the late 1980s and early 1990s. As one colleague remarked, "Just when I had convinced myself it was prudent to spend more on a new house than I used to think was safe, I had to re-convince myself that it wasn't as safe as I now thought."

Furthermore, as the recession of the early 1990s turned into a raging bull market for the rest of the decade, people had to adjust to the notion that stocks, an investment that was considered to be very risky, were now considered by some to be safer long-term than bonds. This story of value-driven behavior in a fluctuating economy reveals the powerful consequences of holding a covert assumption of linearity when dealing with cyclical phenomenon. It also reminds us that in recent years we have had to rethink many of our values and beliefs in order to implement new management practices such as off-shoring successfully.

- **Formal theories and systems of thought.** It's hard to pick up a newspaper or magazine without finding at least one story challenging some widely held theory that nonetheless continues to guide decisions and actions. Often everyday behavior is based on the tacit acceptance of some formalized belief system, even if people are not aware of the connection. Many people, for example, continue to manage based on management principles that were formulated for the conditions, technologies, markets, labor force, and enterprises of another era. For example, if you ask executives why they want to reorganize, you may still hear: *Because there are too many direct reports and we need to reduce the span-of-control.* This is said as if span-of-control is the major, or only, consideration. It is as if span-of-control were an eternal mathematical principle, rather than a theory developed at the beginning of the twentieth century to help manage low-tech factories of mostly low-skilled workers. The unthinking application of theories developed in one time and place to the issues of a different time and place can be an enormous hidden barrier to getting new ideas and possibilities on-the-table.

- **Paradigms.** The term *paradigm* has come to mean a widely shared, taken-for-granted, set of interrelated assumptions and beliefs that explain something. Thus "span-of-control" is a specific principle within the broader paradigm of "industrial organization and management" developed during the first half of the twentieth century. The discussion of economic decisions regarding debt, savings, and inflation was made within the paradigm of capitalism. Determining which way to look when crossing a street is made within a transportation paradigm (e.g., cars are driven on the right side of the road, trains travel in both directions on tracks, airplanes stop only at airports). Thus a wide range of what people call *reality* is based on unexamined, and therefore covert, beliefs and assumptions.

  Often a taken-for-granted paradigm is recognized only when it is confronted by another paradigm or there has been a challenge to one or more of its central assumptions. For example, many organizations today are having their industrial-age paradigms challenged by globalization and the new information technologies. At such times people realize just how many of their assumptions have been covertly determined by the previously hidden paradigm.

- **Organizational and societal cultures.** At the most fundamental level of an organization or society are the taken-for-granted assumptions (about people, time, relationships, the environment) that create the dominant worldview of the social system. The beliefs and assumptions contained within an organizational or societal culture may be so ingrained that it is almost impossible to conceive of a world where another set of beliefs or assumptions are possible. As a corollary, the practices, customs, and ways of doing work based on those beliefs and assumptions are similarly unassailable. When challenged by another worldview that is based on an alternative set of assumptions, members of the focal system often react as if "reality" itself were being questioned, or a whole "way of life" endangered.

Recall the initial reactions of Western corporations to the challenge from Japanese management practices in the 1980s. Eventually the most successful of those practices were adapted and adopted (e.g., TQM). This happened, however, only after many discussions about how practices based in Japanese culture were not useable in Western companies.

At the Precision Corporation, one of the most powerful injunctions was *Never make a mistake!* This was based on an unspoken cultural assumption that the organization would cease to exist if there was any kind of error or mistake in its products and services. Over the years, every aspect of the organization had been developed to guard against errors. Elaborate manuals, detailed SOPs, by-the-book training, and more had been implemented. All behaviors were conservative and risk-adverse. All work processes had checkers in every work unit and at every level of the organization. This was considered normal, and necessary for success. After all, the organization had been around for more than 75 years, so obviously the strategy of protecting against making a mistake worked! When a new executive hired from the outside suggested "re-engineering" work processes to eliminate some of the multiple reviews, the reaction was fierce and hostile: *It's not possible! Are you crazy, you'll endanger the whole organization!*

When the executive suggested that instead of twenty reviews maybe only ten or twelve were needed, the response was: *You're out of touch with reality.* The executive slowly came to realize that the entire culture of the organization with respect to never making a mistake, and all the systems, policies, practices, and procedures built upon that culture, would have to be challenged in order to successfully re-engineer any of the work processes. This was more than the executive had originally envisioned, but certainly explained why it had been so hard to put redesigning the review processes on-the-table.

Challenging Beliefs in the Prism

In each of the earlier examples, some belief or set of beliefs contained within the prism of the focal system was covertly impacting behavior and action. Until such beliefs are challenged, allowing the system to re-think the situation, significant change is unlikely. Ways to help a system challenge potentially inappropriate or dysfunctional values, beliefs, and assumptions include:

1. Visit or import another belief system.

2. Use cognitive dissonance.

3. Dispute the value, belief, or assumption.

Visit or Import Another Belief System

Introducing a person who thinks "differently" to the focal system—especially if the person has legitimacy and status—creates an opportunity for previously taken-for-granted assumptions to be exposed and confronted. Bringing in an expert speaker may serve the same purpose, although it may not be as effective as introducing a high-profile person from the same industry, background, or situation. Visiting a successful outside organization to see, hear, feel, and think about how they do things can also be a powerful way to expose people to alternative possibilities. Seeing an organization that is in a similar situation doing things differently because of different beliefs can powerfully reveal taken-for-granted assumptions and stimulate much-needed rethinking. The focal system that "stays at home" remains within a setting that supports and reinforces its prevailing prism. Being in "another land" often triggers confronting "the way things are" beliefs and assumptions.

Cognitive Dissonance

Cognitive dissonance is a term used to describe the difficulty of acting one way while thinking another (Festinger, 1957). For example, environmental researchers asked people swimming in a lake if they thought the lake was polluted. At every beach around the lake the answer was the same: *Yes, the lake is polluted—but at other beaches, not here.* When your thoughts and actions are not congruent, the dissonance creates tension that motivates you to bring your thoughts and actions into alignment. If I am swimming in a polluted lake, I need to believe that where I am is not polluted. If a focal system believes it is dangerous to talk openly about feelings, then feelings won't be expressed. Conversely, if feelings start to be discussed openly, then the belief that talking about feelings is dangerous may need to be modified in order to maintain congruence (e.g., it may come to be considered appropriate to talk about feelings, but only during stressful events that are impacting the lives of employees).

One way to challenge limiting beliefs and assumptions is to lead the focal system to act differently. *Acting* in new ways increases the dissonance they feel and, to reduce the tension, they will begin *thinking* in new ways. In one organization, collaborative efforts were always difficult and people tended to work alone because of an unspoken belief that *You can't trust other people in a crunch*. After a number of collaborative efforts were intentionally created by management and carefully supported to ensure visible success, people came to believe: *You can trust people you know to get a job done, especially when there is a lot of management support to do it.*

Disputing Ways of Thinking

Disputing is the process of challenging the veracity, utility, or relevance of a value, belief, or assumption in a particular situation. Only when deeply ingrained beliefs in its prism are confronted and shown to be no longer relevant will a focal system begin to rethink what it is doing. One method of disputing is based on the work of Albert Ellis (1962). The accompanying table uses the "no mistakes" organization previously discussed as an example. As the table demonstrates, when taken-for-granted assumptions in a focal system's prism are challenged there is an opportunity for rethinking to occur. This encourages new beliefs and resulting behaviors to emerge.

Method for Disputing Beliefs to Stimulate Rethinking

Step	Example
1. Identify the focal value, belief, or assumption.	1. The organization will cease to exist if even one mistake is made in our product/service.
2. What data exist to dispute or disprove this value, belief, or assumption?	2. The X service was delivered late with 10 errors. In fact, no products or services have ever been delivered with no mistakes in the past 10 years.
3. What data exist to support or prove this value, belief, or assumption?	3. We get disapproving comments and negative feedback when we make mistakes, but realistically our survival is not threatened.
4. What are the bad things that could happen if we violated this value, belief, or assumption?	4. We would get a lot of negative feedback. We'd have to clean up our act and reduce the number of errors. Our reputation would suffer. If it happened over a long period of time we could be in real danger.
5. What are the good things that could happen if we violated this value, belief, or assumption?	5. We could reduce the amount of time it takes to deliver our product/services. People would be less stressed out. We wouldn't be constantly checking on each other. We could reduce one or more levels of control.
6. Can we still rationally hold this value, belief, or assumption?	6. Maybe not.

Worksheet for Rethinking Patterns

Figuring out what kinds of unacknowledged prism beliefs may be impacting performance is challenging because these beliefs are normally out-of-awareness. We need a way to get at the beliefs and assumptions that are leading to the unwanted behavior. The accompanying worksheet offers a simple way to identify limiting beliefs and their consequences. You can use it to guide inquiry into the prisms of a focal system.

Worksheet for Rethinking Prism Patterns

Select a situation you want to explore, then complete the following cues.

1. **When:** (Describe the trigger situation or event)

2. **I/we assume** (tell ourselves): (automatic thoughts, beliefs, assumptions, "tapes" evoked by the trigger event)

3. **And I/we feel:** (emotional reactions like happy, sad, angry, frightened, anxious)

4. **So what I/we do is:** (behavioral actions and responses to the trigger event)

5. **And the result is:** (outcomes for you, others, the situation)

Key Questions

- Where and when did these thoughts or assumptions originate?

- Do they realistically apply in this situation, or are they an old, "habitual" reaction?

- Are you getting the results you want? If not, what results would you prefer?

- What are some alternative, more realistic assumptions?

Now look at the example of a completed worksheet that was used to help someone recognize and rethink patterns of interactions with their superior. It shows that one way to invite a focal system to change a particular behavior pattern is by helping it to rethink the previously hidden beliefs that are limiting possibilities and performance.

Example of Completed Worksheet

1. **When:** My boss comes to my office to give me a new assignment.

2. **I assume** (tell myself): It's a waste of time because the boss already has the answer and knows exactly what s/he wants to do. What I say or do doesn't matter.

3. **And I feel:** Angry, frustrated, defensive, and wanting to run away.

4. **So what I do is:** Tell the boss I am too busy to do the work or suggest that someone else might be better suited to handle the assignment.

5. **And the result is:** In the short-term, my boss leaves and I don't have to do the time-wasting assignment. I feel less tension and sometimes even that I have "won." In the long-term, my boss may lose confidence in my ability to do the work and eventually move me out of my job or work around me. I wouldn't want that to happen.

Reflection and rethinking: Now that I think about it, my response seems counterproductive. Maybe I should assume that my boss has some ideas about how assignments should be handled and ask what they are. Maybe I'll try that next time and see what happens.

Conclusion

Actions to help a focal system recognize and rethink undesirable behavior patterns linked to the beliefs and assumptions contained within its prism are a powerful way to put new options and possibilities on-the-table. Be sure to remember the focal system is trying the best it can and that most behavior does not arise from innate capabilities but is guided by acquired beliefs in the focal system's prism. These are accessible and, in many cases, changeable.

CHAPTER 8

▶ # Reframing Interventions

Unlike rethinking interventions that directly challenge the usefulness of some belief in the focal system's prism, *reframing* interventions seek to change the way something is interpreted. This is done by finding and altering the belief that the focal system is implicitly using to make sense of a situation. If Pat, the boss of a work group, tells Chris, "You should revise the presentation to have greater impact," several interpretations are possible, depending on how Chris implicitly frames the statement. Leaving aside tone of voice and similar contextual factors, if Chris frames the interaction through the mental model of "autocratic leadership," Pat's comment is likely to be interpreted as an autocratic directive. This then triggers reactions consistent with Chris's beliefs about autocratic leadership. If, on the other hand, the same comment is interpreted through the mental model of "coach," then Pat's statement may be interpreted as a helpful suggestion, leading to a different response from Chris.

Another simple but powerful example of reframing is provided by my colleague Edie Seashore, who when confronted by limiting doubts is quick to add: *Up until now.* So when someone says, on behalf of the organization, "That's not possible. There's no way that can be done . . ." Edie finishes their sentence with ". . . up until now!" Without directly challenging the speaker, Edie reframes the situation to make explicit that the past does not have to dictate the future. This makes possible the search for new options and maintains the presumed desire of the focal system to actually do something. Statements such as "That's not possible" often result from implicit framing beliefs *(What wasn't possible in the past won't be possible in the future)*, or emotions *(Doing that was scary, is scary, and always will be scary)*, or even unconscious dynamics *(Being unable to do something suggests symbolically that we are still dependent children who don't have to be responsible)*. In this instance, reframing the implicit assumption that the future must be the same as the past provides an opportunity to put something on-the-table that had been considered impossible . . . *up until now.*

Reframing, then, involves modifying the way the focal system currently looks at a situation and thereby creating possibilities for new interpretations and behaviors. There is an extensive literature about the theory and practice of reframing, including writings about sensemaking, interpretive schemes, neuro-linguistic programming (NLP), and cognitive linguistics. See the bibliography at the end of this book for further readings.

Basics of Reframing

The accompanying table provides some basic guidelines on how to approach reframing interventions. It is useful to remember that reframing benefits from an artist's eye—and guidelines are not formulas.

Purposes of Reframing

The overall purpose of reframing is to change how something is interpreted through the focal system's prism and thereby create opportunities for new behaviors and courses of action that had not previously been considered. Through reframing it may be possible to do one or more of the following things.

Alter the meaning of an action from a negative to a more positive connotation. As we have learned throughout this book, even clearly needed actions and behaviors won't occur if the focal system believes them to be somehow inappropriate or negative. Consequently, a

Basics of Reframing

Purposes	Understanding another's frame	Six principles
• Alter the meaning of an action from negative toward positive • Rename or rearrange something to encourage more productive action • Provide new ways of experiencing to generate new options • Help empower; don't simply paint a happy face on something	• Step into the other's prism • Understand the other's truth • Be clear about the meaning the other is making of the situation • Discern their positive intent as distinct from their behavior • Know the choices the other believes are available	1. Identify and maintain positive intent 2. Join the system's prism while using your own to create alternatives 3. Identify and address what is necessary to reduce threat 4. Provide new ways of seeing, experiencing, and/or naming the situation 5. Break either/or thinking 6. Work polarities

primary purpose of reframing is to enable the focal system to see how unexplored actions and behaviors might also be appropriate and positive. For example, telling people "no" can be implicitly interpreted as arbitrary or seen as depriving someone of something. It can also be interpreted as being helpful because it implements needed limits that benefit everyone. By helping the focal system reframe its prism beliefs you create options for putting new and different possibilities on-the-table. Remember, you are not trying to make something that is clearly and objectively negative into something positive. That's "spin," not reframing.

Rename or rearrange something such that more productive action is possible. Another purpose of reframing is to help the focal system interpret things in ways that lead to more productive outcomes. For example, Lee is in a project meeting with Leslie, who presents a list of requests for more time and resources. Lee is unsure how to respond because Lee's prism has framed the situation as one in which Leslie is making self-serving demands. Lee doesn't want to cave in to Leslie's agenda and feels both angry and stuck. If the situation were reframed, perhaps after a coaching session or a discussion with a colleague, so that Lee considered it legitimate to rise above the parochial interests of others, more productive options might become possible. Another example of symbolic reframing is changing the seating configuration from antagonists sitting on opposite sides of a rectangular table to mixed groups at round tables. This does not change the agenda, or the interests in the room. It does, however, symbolically reframe the meeting from a negotiation session to a problem-solving meeting, thereby implicitly encouraging more collaborative behavior.

Provide new ways for the focal system to generate new and positive actions. Sometimes a focal system's prism frames things in ways that reinforce negative or self-limiting beliefs. For example, following several quarters of downward-trending results, a sales manager became lost in negativity and unable to think about productive actions to take: *There is nothing I can do. I just don't seem to have what it takes. Maybe they'll get someone else in here who will do a better job.*

Here the framing of "failure" was so strong the manager was unable to see that results had actually improved in some markets for some products. When a respected colleague suggested the manager review the results for positive as well as negative news, the initial response was: *It's all bad news.* Later, however, the manager decided to re-look at the results for any positive news, and was now able to see some areas for action that had previously been ignored. One way to experience poor results in the marketplace is to see yourself as repudiated and a failure. Another way is to see the results as useful feedback. Focusing on what's missing (the glass half empty) can deprive a system of building upon its assets (the glass is half full). . . *up until now.* Another purpose of reframing, therefore, is to help a focal system see things in ways that will generate positive responses.

Help empower—don't just paint a happy face on a sad situation. Reframing is not the psychological version of spin doctoring, where a positive spin is put on events to enhance someone's image or agenda, usually at another's expense: *No, the president was not intimidated by a two-bit dictator. Great nations are expected to comport themselves with dignity on the world's stage, even if petty clowns do not.* Neither is reframing a way to put a happy face on a sad situation: *Gee, we lost the big* contract. *That's great—it will give us the time to improve our operations.* Instead, reframing is ultimately about creating realistic choices not previously considered by the focal system. This means that reframing, like all the actions and interventions mentioned in this book, is done only for the purposes of helping the focal system achieve its objectives. To do this requires clear and careful attunement to the focal system in question.

Understanding Another's Frame

A simple truth underlies the essential requirement for a successful reframing intervention: In order to reframe successfully you must first understand the other's existing frame. To understand another's frame requires the ability to:

- See, hear, feel, and think about the world as they do. By asking questions, listening, and observing the focal system, can you develop a good sense of how it is interpreting the world even if it is different from what you do?

- Discover the beliefs and assumptions contained within the focal system's prism and fully appreciate that those contents are its full reality.

- Clarify the meaning the focal system is making of a situation. Through what prism beliefs and frameworks is it viewing this particular situation? The more you understand the meaning(s) being made, the better able you will be to attempt to reframe some aspect of it.

- Understand the focal system's positive intentions and desired outcomes apart from the results actually being achieved. Whether or not the actions are effective, you start with the assumption that the intention of the focal system is to achieve some positive result as seen through its prism. To do this you need to distinguish between the focal system's current behavior and the positive intentions behind that behavior. A work team might want recognition for its contributions but believe it is inappropriate to blow their own horn. This could lead to a strategy of *Let our work speak for itself*. If the work team's management tends to ignore things unless attention is drawn to them, then the team is likely to experience repeated frustration. Reframing the situation could be helpful to this work team, but it is critical to understand that what is desired is acknowledgement (their positive intention), not just a better way to make the work speak for itself (their behavioral strategy). You might be able to reframe the act of providing information to others from blowing our own horn to: *It's important to keep people fully informed so they can better support us.*

- Explore what options the focal system believes are available, or feasible. All too frequently focal systems see few choices other than to continue doing what they've been doing and hope things will get better, because *There is nothing else to do*. And, from their prism and experience, they are absolutely correct. Reframing to generate new options may then be needed.

Six Principles of Reframing

Six principles to guide successful reframing grow out of the preceding discussion.

1. Identify and maintain the positive intent of the focal system. As discussed in Chapter 5, one of the keys to working with covert processes is to assume the focal system is doing the best it can (given its experience and prism), regardless of the actual results achieved. In short, for purposes of diagnosis and action, you initially assume most behavior is intended to achieve some positive outcome for the focal system. As an outside observer you might wonder why the focal system engages in such ineffective or even self-destructive acts, but it's your job to identify what the focal system is trying to achieve.

What is the desired outcome? Better results? Improved performance? A different emotional state? Sometimes, when there is enough safety and trust, just asking what someone really wants provides enough information. Whatever the desired outcome, reframing interventions should maintain the positive intent of the focal system while altering the limiting frame in order to generate new options.

Reframing interventions work when they help the focal system generate new ways to achieve what it needs. Reframing will be experienced as manipulative if you reframe things to achieve outcomes not desired by the focal system. If the focal system really wants safe results, regardless of the apparently risky behavior being exhibited, attempting to reframe the situation so it can take better risks will not work. Helping an individual clarify desired outcomes and then reframing as "safe and assured methods lead to safe and assured results" might have a better chance of success, while providing some new possibilities to consider.

2. **Join the focal system in its prism while using your own to create options.** Successful reframing requires the ability to step into another's prism and see, hear, feel and experience things from their point of view. Without this empathic ability it is difficult—or at best guess-work—to identify the focal system's positive intent separate from its observable behavior. Stepping into another prism, however, does not mean leaving your own behind. Instead, it means simultaneously and nonjudgmentally holding your own and the other's point of view. This allows you to have a good sense of what the focal system is seeking to achieve, the limitations and choices from its point of view, and the awareness of untested possibilities from your own prism. For example, in the work group wanting recognition, you need to understand that they want recognition, but believe they have no options beyond blowing their own horns, which they are unwilling to do. From your own prism, you may know several other options are possible.

In the first place, blowing your own horn is not the only way to get attention, although through this work group's prism it appears to be. Second, in your experience you know that sending useful information upward can be seen as helpful and not self-serving. Thus your prism is used as a source of ideas to help reframe the situation. If your prism perspective is not brought to bear and you simply join the system in its prism, empathy and support are possible, but new options will be precluded by the existing frame of reference.

3. **Identify and address what is necessary to reduce threat.** Fear and anxiety are primary breeding grounds for covert processes and major impediments to creativity and empowerment. One reason a focal

system will stay stuck in self-defeating or self-limiting behavior patterns is because the results are safely predictable. While an outsider might observe that the results are rather meager, the focal system could respond that at least they are predictable and they can cope with them. For some focal systems, to try significantly different behavior is to risk everything.

Because reframing creates options for new behavior, even a well-intended reframing intervention could be experienced as a threat by raising previously unthinkable ideas. Obviously, actions to minimize any perceived risk must be part of a successful reframing intervention. Suppose members of a work team are reluctant to discuss areas for improvement directly with the team leader because they are implicitly framing the situation as giving unwanted criticism to the boss. With that framing, providing such information would certainly induce anxiety.

To reframe this situation successfully you would need to address two dimensions. One involves reframing information about areas for improvement from "unwanted criticism" to "helpful ways for everyone to do better." The other dimension involves addressing the sense of threat. This could possibly be done by reframing providing such information as "team sharing to improve performance" rather than "direct and unsolicited criticism of the boss." In essence, you need to reframe in ways that help the focal system perceive that the new behaviors are both possible and realistically "safe enough" to be carried out.

4. Provide new ways of seeing, experiencing, or naming the situation. The purpose of reframing is to alter the interpretation of something enough to make new behavioral options possible. Helping a focal system see something in a new light, feel different about it, or define it more usefully is the essence of reframing. Helping a focal system see something differently includes encouraging it to look at things from a different perspective. For example, if two individuals are locked in a win-lose conflict, asking them *How critical would these issues be if you were looking down from the moon?* might reframe sufficiently to open up additional options. Asking a work team to try using playful behaviors because they are a proven aid to creative problem-solving might invite even the most serious, task-driven work group to "seriously" give it a try.

Renaming something to highlight previously ignored aspects can dramatically shift attitudes. What it is might remain the same, but what it *means* may be changed enough to elicit new behavior. Renaming the glass from "half empty" to "half full" does not change the size of the glass or the amount of liquid; it does change how we experience the glass and its contents.

Remember that it is vital for you to understand the situation from the perspective of the focal system. Otherwise you risk perceptions of spin doctoring, or worse. Attempts by management to influence employee attitudes by renaming "downsizing" as "rightsizing" still register as layoffs to most employees. Given what is at stake, renaming alone is insufficient. Employees' attitudes will be more positively impacted by concrete actions such as retraining programs, placement services, types of "packages," and the like. The renaming of downsizing to rightsizing, however, could have a positive impact on the people *planning* the actions. For them, the rightsizing reframing could create new ways of interpreting their assignment: Downsizing frames things in terms of cuts, reductions, and loss, while rightsizing includes images of becoming fit and responsive.

5. **Break either/or thinking.** It is not unusual for a focal system to become stuck in either/or thinking: My way or your way; the right answer or the wrong answer; victory or humiliation; our point of view (which is totally good) or their point of view (which is totally bad). This way of thinking reduces all possibilities to two exaggerated and potentially extreme positions, only one of which is even remotely acceptable from the focal system's point of view. In such cases, reframing the situation to allow more than two options on-the-table is an important intervention. Understanding the underlying positive intent of the focal system is critical. Does the focal system want to simply win an encounter or does it want to achieve some other outcome, such as improved customer service? If so, can the situation be reframed from a win-lose mentality and at the same time highlight new possibilities to achieve other desired outcomes? Consider a customer-service unit at war with a sales unit over customer expectations of product service: *Yes, we could go for a knockout victory over sales on this one, but that would lead to later retaliation; or we could capitulate to what they are doing, but then we'd be in a no-win situation. Suppose instead we formed an alliance*

with them to provide "service that sells." If we could successfully pull it off that would help everyone—them, us, and the customers. When successful, breaking either/or thinking provides an impetus to search for new options and be open to new possibilities.

6. Work polarities. Another way of reframing polarized ways of thinking that limit possibilities is by working the polarities. One of the primary ways we can understand something is by contrasting it with its apparent opposite: *This is more because that is less. That is a smart decision because the other choice would be stupid.* Any focal system at least partly defines itself and its actions through comparisons, either explicit or implicit. Frequently those comparisons become loaded; the focal system idolizes one side of the polarity while demonizing the other:

> A focal system might protect its own positive image by characterizing others negatively: *We are well-informed and they are ignorant!* Sometimes a focal system may perpetuate its own negative image by idealizing another's: *Their department has enlightened leadership, while we have clueless, out-of-date managers.* When a polarity is "loaded," choices are limited because the other (position, party, possibility) is framed as unacceptable. Reframing one or both aspects of any polarity as more neutral, mutually acceptable, or just different, legitimates consideration of previously unacceptable choices. It might be unacceptable to work with someone who is stupid, but all right to work with someone who is naïve or "just learning." Because we see ourselves as "awkward" and others as "polished," we might hold back. If we saw ourselves as "enthusiastic learners" we might be more willing to contribute around others we consider more polished.

When your reframing intervention has been successful, the focal system should experience the situation it is dealing with in several new ways. First, they may have an increased sense of empowerment that derives from a greater sense of control due to awareness of more choices. Second, increased confidence and emotional well-being can arise when a situation defined as limiting and negative shifts to one with more positive possibilities. Finally, increased energy and more flexibility result from the reframed situation.

Reframing in Action

My first example not only reframes an individual's prism, but gives a sense of the way recognizing, rethinking, and reframing might unfold in the moment (Marshak, 2004). The example comes from a situation where I was coaching an internal human resources development (HRD) consultant. Information provided in *italics* conveys scene setting information, commentary, or my internal thoughts at the time.

Jane is a well-regarded internal HRD consultant working on a difficult change initiative. I was working with her as a shadow consultant/ coach. The following abbreviated excerpt is from a conversation we had near the beginning of our working together.

Bob: Jane, tell me more about this new change project you are working on.

Jane: Well, it's a very challenging assignment. There isn't much support for the change—I am really out there on my own.

Bob: Is there a sponsor for the change? Who are you working for?

Jane: I'm working for John C. and I don't want to let him down. I need to get out there and lead the way despite all the resistance.

Bob: You sound alone in this . . .

Jane: I'm very much alone. I'm kinda out there ahead of everyone else, dealing with all the resistance and attacks from everyone opposed to the change. It's a very lonely position, but someone has to do it.

I was starting to hear a symbolic theme with word images similar to those of someone on military reconnaissance deep in enemy territory who is "on point." Being "on point" is being out in front of everyone else in the most dangerous and vulnerable position. I wondered if Jane was implicitly framing the situation in this way and what impacts that might have for how she saw her choices. I had heard military images many times, but more typically from men, so I was tentative about this initial hunch and decided to get more background.

Bob: By the way, Jane, have you ever been in the military or worked in a military organization?

Jane: Well, if you count my family, yes. I come from a military family—both my father and older brother are in the army.

Learning that Jane had a military background, I decided to explore the way she was experiencing her assignment by asking questions that would elicit more insights into her way of seeing things. In short, I wanted to learn more about her prism.

Bob: So, I understand that you are out on this difficult assignment. Tell me, how did you get this assignment?

Jane: I got it from John C.

Bob: Hmmm. Well, did John C. call you in and give you the assignment? Were you recommended by others? Did you volunteer? How did it happen?

Jane: I knew someone needed to do it, so I went to John C. and told him I'd be willing to be out in front and take the fire because his change initiative is so important.

Hearing Jane talk in terms of "someone needing to do it" and "being in front and taking the fire" made me more confident about my hunch that military framing might covertly be at work. I wondered if Jane was operating from a military "on point" framework that was out of her conscious awareness. I tested this hunch by trying to step into her prism and empathize with her way of experiencing the world. I also began testing possible reframings that might give Jane more options while maintaining her intent of making an important contribution.

Bob: Wow, it must be pretty scary to be out in front of everyone; that's a pretty vulnerable position.

Jane: (pausing) It is. It is very scary, but I don't think about it because it needs to be done and someone has to do it.

Bob: So you have more or less volunteered to be out on point on this assignment?

Jane: Yes, pretty much so. I figured I was the best person to do it and I didn't want to let John C. down. I owed him my loyalty, and the change initiative is very important.

I decided to be more direct with Jane and to test one way the situation might be reframed to give her more support. My initial approach would be to see how Jane reacted to a reframing of the options in the "on point" image without directly confronting the image. I also made a mental note to see how extensively this image, or military images in general, were influencing the way Jane experiences the world. At some future time this image might need to be reflected back to Jane to see whether it may be unconsciously limiting her options in other situations.

Bob: You describe yourself as out in front, all alone. Do you have any help or support? Have you asked for any?

Jane: Well, no, it's my job to take the lead in this.

Bob: Couldn't you ask John C. for support to back you up or provide better cover? After all you are on a mission to advance his agenda.

Jane: Well, I volunteered . . .

Bob: . . . for a suicide mission?

Jane: (frown) Well no . . . (now smiling) although sometimes it feels that way!

I suggested a specific reframing to see if asking for support, or setting up the situation in a more favorable way, was an option for Jane. In essence, I wanted to reframe the all-or-nothing way she was interpreting her "volunteer mission" to allow the possibility of asking for help.

Bob: I don't know John C., but it seems to me that if you are on an important mission for him it would be all right to ask for as much support and help as possible . . .

Jane: Even if I volunteered? Wouldn't that be pushy or out-of-line?

Bob: Again, I don't know John C., but I think it is completely appropriate to tell him what is needed for a successful change project and to ask for everything you need to ensure that you are effective in making his change initiative a success. You know, he has some obligation of loyalty to you too. You are advancing his initiative. If it's something he wants, then it should be something for which he is willing to provide strong support.

Jane: (tentatively) Hmmm . . . well, maybe I could ask for some help. I could really use it.

Bob: If you did ask him for support, what would you need?

Jane: (laughing) Lots! For starters I need . . .

At this point, the conversation was reframed into exploring what was needed for a successful mission—and underscoring the acceptability of requesting it from John C. A more confrontational reframing intervention would have been to challenge the military imagery that seemed to frame the way Jane was experiencing her situation. That actually occurred in a later meeting when "dangerous military mission" imagery continued to pervade Jane's descriptions of her work on the change initiative.

Other possible interventions could have occurred in the shadow coaching relationship between Jane and me. There are also other interpretations of what might have been going on within Jane—including, perhaps, nonmilitary interpretations. The purpose of presenting this case is not to suggest exactly what should be done or how certain phrases should be interpreted, but to give a realistic example of recognizing, rethinking, and especially reframing in action.

Let's look at a second example, where the organizing frame for a change intervention was questioned and reframed. The episode happened during a meeting with C.J., the executive director and Francis, the chief engineer of Global Solutions, a mid-sized software company.

Global Solutions was engaged in a change initiative to make the company less "bureaucratic" and to encourage operating across organizational boundaries in cross-departmental teams. C.J., Francis, and I met to develop ways to advance that initiative.

The change effort was bogged down among middle managers who either didn't "get it" or were reluctant to give up direct control over their people, projects, and budgets. C.J. suggested putting together a two-hour briefing on what was needed followed by a one-hour Q&A session for the middle managers. Francis supported the idea and encouraged making the session as short as possible because "We don't want to waste our people's time."

I had worked with Global Solutions for a number of years and understood their culture pretty well, so I wasn't too surprised. Nonetheless, I didn't think the proposed briefing had any chance of helping, so I interjected that I thought the middle managers needed to be engaged in much more substantial ways. Perhaps we should consider a series of meetings so that middle managers working in groups could discuss factors impacting the proposed changes.

Both C.J. and Francis challenged my reasoning: *Our people are really smart, they don't need all that. Doing that small-group stuff is like playing kiddie games. They don't need a lot of time, they're quick studies. Only really smart people work here and we don't want to insult their intelligence by taking all that time.* Both the direct and symbolic nature of these comments made it clear that they were framing the situation as one where smart people needed only to be quickly informed about what to do, and not much more. My response was intended to challenge that assumption while reframing the situation: *You often describe this company as being like a college campus or an elite graduate school. What I can't figure out is why so many really smart people just can't get it. Maybe they need a remedial management course. Maybe they are engineers having a hard time in a poetry course. Maybe they haven't had the prerequisites for this new course. All I know is that acting as if they are really bright students doesn't seem to fit the facts of the situation.*

After a short pause, C.J. commented: *You know, maybe we do need to bring them along more slowly. I'll bet none of them has had any management training in people skills. What can you expect?*

Francis then chimed in, suggesting: *Well, we could put them through a series of workshops, building-block fashion.*

In this episode the initial implicit framing of the situation by C. J. and Francis seemed pretty clear from their metaphors and word images. Unlike the situation with Jane, where her military framing was not initially challenged, in this instance the "really smart student" frame was directly questioned. At the same time, the overall "students learning something new" frame was maintained. What was questioned and reframed was what kinds of students they were and what they were learning.

Conclusion

The prisms through which individuals, groups, and organizations view the world are powerful determinants of their behavior and action. Knowing how to work with a focal system's prism thus becomes a key skill for change agents. In particular, the following abilities are critical:

1. The ability to diagnose, decode, and develop good hunches about the contents of a focal system's prism.

2. The ability to view and understand the world through another's prism while being able to hold onto your own prism and point of view.

3. The ability to address the frameworks that are creating meaning in a specific situation—not just what people are saying and doing, but the implicit frames that are guiding the way something is being understood and acted upon.

4. The ability to recognize, rethink, and/or reframe constraining contents of your own and others' prisms.

Reframing aspects of a focal system's prism creates possibilities for significant behavioral change. By altering a framework, new possibilities can be placed on-the-table and openly engaged. If you are unable to help a focal system recognize, rethink, and reframe its prism, you will constantly confront invisible barriers to your efforts. This is especially true when working on fundamental changes that confront deeply held, but usually out-of-awareness beliefs, values, and assumptions.

CHAPTER 9

Rethinking Organizational Politics

In earlier chapters, the Covert Processes Model was used as a way to explain the existence of covert dynamics that impact organizational change. The logical, rational, **reasons** (the case for change) for an organizational initiative are generally seen as legitimate and therefore put on–the-table for overt engagement. However, reasons are not necessarily enough to keep the change initiative on-the-table, or to ensure that covert dynamics don't block it.

Inspirations, the values-based and visionary aspirations of people, may go unexpressed if considered too good to be true, thereby depriving the change initiative of a significant source of positive energy and commitment. Similarly **emotions**, the affective and reactive feelings of people about the change, may be considered inappropriate to express openly, and therefore be denied and hidden under-the-table. The impacts of these emotional reactions, however, may turn up in other, more covert ways.

Mindsets, the guiding beliefs and assumptions that exist in the prisms of people, can also serve as blinders and filters, potentially blocking consideration of new possibilities. Finally, anxiety-based and unconscious defenses may lead to repressed or untapped **psychodynamics** that could impact the change initiative. That covers five of the six dimensions of organizational change that were first introduced in Chapter 1, but what about individual and group interests, or **politics**?

Perspectives on Politics

Whether political processes are hidden or acknowledged during organizational change depends on the prisms involved. When the use of power is seen as inappropriate in making decisions about organizational initiatives, then politics is typically hidden and thus poorly observed or considered. To be sure, there are some political moves and hidden deals that are intentionally covert and can surprise or blindside the most alert organizational player. However, in my experience, even more political behavior in organizations is not addressed mainly because it is somehow considered to be wrong. Instead, political behavior is considered to be questionable, illegitimate, or inappropriate, and people refuse to engage in it or, sometimes, even to see it. Although I have observed this phenomenon for more than thirty years in all types of organizations, it still puzzles me, due no doubt to the contents of my prism.

My Own Prism

My prism has been influenced to varying degrees by my education and my early career working as an analyst (and later an executive) in a federal food and agricultural science agency. My undergraduate degree is in political science and my masters and doctoral degrees are in public administration. During almost nine years of government service I was constantly involved in organizational, policy, and budgetary matters that required a keen appreciation for the political dimension of organizations. Governmental agencies, although run according to good administrative principles, are also implementers of the broader political process. They are *inherently* political in nature. Consequently, it was second nature for me to look at things through my prism with political as well as scientific, organizational, and management eyes. Consideration of the interests of those directly impacted by possible changes in public policy, as well as those of a broad array of interest groups and the public good, was a required part of my job.

This meant thinking about the political interests of the various government entities that would be involved in any significant policy or budgetary shift, including various congressional oversight committees in the House and Senate, White House policy offices, the Office of Management and Budget (OMB), and state legislatures and agencies. Thinking about how to create common ground or forge compromises depending on the relative power of the different stakeholders, as well as what to do during the various stages in the policymaking process, was part of the job.

These kinds of considerations about the political environment of public agencies were also part of my lens for thinking about internal management and organizational changes. What were the interests of the key offices and officials in my agency? What were their sources of power and influence, including connections to outside groups? How were decisions about the topic in question made—including when, where, how, and who. This type of political calculus became part of establishing the context within which sound technical, administrative, management, and organization principles were applied to the issue in question.

Having both management and political lenses in my prism as I viewed organizational dynamics always proved helpful to the work I was doing. It also often differentiated me from both the political officials I worked with, who tended to have only a political lens, and the scientists, who tended to have only a technical lens. I vividly recall a lengthy *What will be our strategy?* discussion with the scientific leader of a research area targeted by OMB for drastic budget cuts. Our orientations, and what we would consider putting on-the-table as possible actions, couldn't have been more different. I wanted to pursue a variety of actions and strategies that recognized both the power and political orientation of OMB; accordingly, I suggested strategies to bring other actors and factors into the process as a way to change the political dynamics in the hope of reducing the size of the proposed cuts. My scientist colleague could only say over and over again that: *OMB shouldn't be making scientific decisions. They don't understand science. They are wrong, so we shouldn't try to negotiate with them.* And finally, *They will be sorry when we have a famine!*

From my prism, the political fact that we were experiencing huge food surpluses and large budget deficits meant little or nothing to someone whose prism said making scientific funding decisions should be based solely on consideration of what is good science. To do otherwise would be unacceptable, illegitimate, or inappropriate and should not be put on-the-table.

Two Perspectives

In both public and private organizations, the degree to which politics is, or should be, involved in organizational change seems to have two dominant perspectives. One is that organizations should be rational-logical instruments; the other is that organizations, like all social collectives, are inherently political systems. The rational-logical perspective has been the implicit view in most organizations and management textbooks since the early 1900s (Weber, 1946). From this perspective, those given hierarchical authority should make decisions using technical knowledge, sound management principles, and logic to advance the best interests of the organization. Decisions based on position or personal power are considered illegitimate, inappropriate, or unacceptable and must be guarded against. Often, as with my scientist colleague, the rational-logical perspective makes it difficult to think politically in an organizational context. It sometimes leads to an inability to see political phenomena even when in plain sight because of the filters in the focal system's prism. Relying on making the case for change is another part of the "organizations are rational-logical instruments" paradigm.

Despite the dominance of the rational-logical perspective, some have always seen organizations as inherently de facto political systems. The perspective of "organizations as political systems," expects that there will be uses of power by a range of actors to advance their own interests. Decisions result from emergent processes wherein constituencies bring their own needs, interests, perspectives, and methods of influence to bear in pursuit of their desired outcomes. Such political processes include both individual power and influence and aspects of coalition behavior. From this perspective, organizational change is a political event—or even a political campaign—where the interests of some constituencies end up being advanced over those of others. Downsizing, outsourcing, reorganizations, changes in product priorities, and shifts in strategy all have impacts on various officials, offices, and employee groups. While the rational-logical perspective may be a desirable ideal, the reality is that to ignore the political dimension of organizations is to ignore obvious and powerful dynamics that will impact any change initiative. When operating from this prism, political behavior is considered to be legitimate, appropriate, and acceptable—or at least to be *expected*—during organizational change. Such a perspective encourages active seeing and thinking about the political dimensions of change. It also encourages putting political considerations on-the-table during change planning and implementation discussions.

Applying Both Political and Management Perspectives

Although the two perspectives about politics in organizations may be dichotomous, we must acknowledge that *both* apply in any change initiative. We must consider the rational-logical case for change, but we must also see the interests and political processes that inherently will be part of any attempt to modify the status quo. The good news is that including both in our prisms about organizational change allows both to be put on-the-table and openly engaged. It also means using each one to inform the other: *How might the political realities of the situation influence our case for change? How can we use the case for change to influence organizational politics?*

Such a combined approach will likely necessitate a shift in change planning. We need to shift from an emphasis on finding the objectively "right" answer to an appreciation for building commitment to an acceptable, *feasible* answer. In many cases, this will require reframing some prism beliefs about politically acceptable answers being nothing more than watered-down compromises.

Operating from a Political Perspective

For a range of reasons, many leaders, staff specialists, and especially consultants treat power and political processes as if they were an evil force operating in organizations: Power is to be feared because it can demolish you and your change effort; politics is to be avoided because if you see or engage in it you will be contaminated. Neither is generally talked about approvingly. The old superstition is still strong: *To say the name of an evil spirit is to invoke its presence.* This orientation ensures that most of an organization's political dynamics remain covert during change planning and implementation. If, however, you rethink or reframe your mindset, it will become necessary and appropriate to operate from a political perspective, in addition to other perspectives, during change planning and management (Greiner and Schein, 1988). This will encourage a wider range of considerations to be put on-the-table and engaged.

Power

Over the years I have been struck by the profound ambivalence or even antagonism toward power expressed by many of the people involved in organizational change efforts. Most surprising is the lack of awareness that the effective and appropriate use of power is a *necessary* component of successful organizational change. This may arise from a confusion between what power is versus how power is used.

When power is implicitly defined as "aggression against" or "resistance in defense of" something, then the focus becomes how to neutralize, combat, or defend against it. This leads to anti-aggression or anti-power orientations that view any use of power—by anyone—as dangerous, and to behaviors intended to block the use of power. Paradoxically, power is used to negate power, resulting in a less "power-full" focal system overall.

Without power, the impetus to change is left vulnerable to the competing factors, forces, and personalities in the focal system. How can you expect to be a change agent, to lead or facilitate change, without power? Beyond rationally making the case for change, it is obvious that power is needed to plan and implement organizational changes effectively.

Politics

Politics is the process of people using power to achieve their preferred outcomes. This definition emphasizes that organizational politics is a process whereby decisions are made and outcomes realized. How that happens and who is involved are two of the key aspects of the political process, both in governments and organizations. Some questions to consider include:

- Which people make the decisions? (top management, those impacted, a representative task force, the board of directors)

- What types of power can be used to influence outcomes? (expert information, rewards and inducements, someone's official position, threats, coercive pressure)

- What processes are used to make decisions? (top-down, participatory, consensus, dialogue meetings)

- Whose and what preferred outcomes are considered legitimate, or are most valued? (shareholders, top management, the union, rank-and-file employees, sales, manufacturing, human resources, finance, global, domestic)

In an organizational change effort, these dimensions help indicate what the political process will be. For example, one political process could be that important changes are decided by an inner circle of top managers and then implemented using top-down, logical persuasion methods to advance the interests of shareholders. If this is an organization's political process, you might be alert to the possibility of countervailing power seeking to have a broader range of actors and interests involved in a more participatory process. Of course, participatory forms of decision-making could be opposed by those in the organization whose interests are best served by a less open process. The way any organizational change is planned and implemented involves organizational power and politics inherently. To think otherwise is to leave your change effort vulnerable.

Organizational Perspectives

When acting from a political perspective, keep in mind that different actors will have different orientations to both the substance and processes of change based on their fields of experience and prisms. This goes beyond asking yourself *Who are the stakeholders and what do they want?* It includes consideration of the differing mindsets of the organizational players and how those mindsets may make collaboration more difficult.

A good example of differing mindsets based on organizational position and responsibilities comes from my days working in the federal government. In the United States system of public administration, government agencies are headed by political leaders with career civil servants reporting to them. The political leadership, therefore, have not only top management mindsets but also political mindsets regarding the programs and policies for which they are responsible. Agency heads will have been appointed by whatever president and party won the most recent presidential election and they are expected to be loyal to the winning political party's agenda. The civil servants reporting to them, on the other hand, are responsible for the technical, managerial, and administrative aspects of the programs assigned to them. They are expected to follow both the political leadership and sound professional practices. To this mix we add various staff specialists who advise both the political and civil service leadership based on their areas of expertise. During significant organizational or policy changes these disparate actors must somehow work together for a change initiative to be successful. This is made more difficult when there is little recognition or understanding of the differing mindsets involved. The accompanying table compares the prisms and mindsets of an HR staff specialist, career manager, and political official as they think about organizational change.

To whatever degree differing mindsets exist, they increase the difficulty of collaborating for change and may raise trust concerns as well. This leads in turn to covert dynamics. It is essential to understand that change *always* has a political dimension, whether in the public or private sectors, and that the interests of various organizational actors must be recognized and engaged constructively. If differing mindsets are seen as being driven by inappropriate, illegitimate, or questionable considerations, or by self-interest, it makes implementing *any* change more difficult. The perspectives of significant organizational actors and components must be acknowledged and addressed, to at least some degree, in order to secure their cooperation and support.

HRD, Career Service, and Political Perspectives

Dimension	HR staff specialist	Career manager	Political official
Who decides	"Everyone involved should collaborate."	"We are responsible for the decision based on our technical judgment and the best interests of the program."	"We decide because we won the election. To the victor go the spoils."
Decision Process	Participatory and consensual	Reasoned analysis and conclusions by the experts	Majority vote, then implementing the winner's agenda
Time frame	3 to 5 years	Next budget cycle (1 to 3 years)	Next election (2 to 4 years)
Change is:	Good. Positive. Improvement.	Threatening to fiduciary responsibility to provide stability and caretake the program in the public interest	Opportunity to advance our party's policy agenda and/ or undo the losing party's agenda
Purpose of change	Enhance human and organizational potential	Enhance program and organizational ends	Enhance political agenda, influence, and electability
How others are seen	"Neither careerists nor politicians consider the best interests of the people and the total system."	"Neither politicians nor HR specialists consider the best interests of the program."	"Neither careerists nor HR specialists consider the best interests of the electorate and the winning political agenda."

Seeing Organizations as Political Systems

To better work with the political dimension in organizational change, you need to be able to think about organizations as political as well as rational-logical systems. The following discussion draws on ideas from political science to present a diagnostic framework for thinking about organizations as political systems (Ostrom, 1967).

Diagnostic Framework

Eight factors help define the way an organization's political system operates. These factors will help you to analyze the "who, what, why, when, where, and how" of organizational politics and decision-making.

1. **Decision arenas**. This factor considers where, formally and informally, any particular decision is made in an organization. If there is a proposal to change the compensation system, where would the decision be made? In the compensation committee? In the executive committee? Elsewhere? Might the decision be made in one location but need to be sanctioned in several others (e.g., first developed in the compensation committee, then approved by the executive committee, and finally endorsed by the board of directors)? If the decision could be initiated in more than one location, which might be most favorable for the intended change (e.g., perhaps the change would be more likely to be approved if proposed by a group of line managers than by a staff group)? Picking the right arena(s) and avoiding the wrong one(s) is a key strategic political consideration and something to watch for in change planning and implementation.

2. **Degree of participation**. This factor considers who is invited to participate in a decision. The number and type of participants can influence an outcome, and modifications to either are important political choices. In some organizations, participation is restricted to high-status players, while in others broad participation is encouraged. Changing the degree of participation will distribute advantages and disadvantages to different organizational actors and interests. Because any change in the degree of participation in an organization will rearrange the existing power configuration, overt or covert resistance is to be expected.

3. **Decision rounds**. This factor considers how many rounds of decision-making will be necessary to achieve implementation. It is also related to decision arenas because a change in arena may signal another round of decision-making. For any organizational

change there may be multiple rounds of decision-making: first a decision to study the issue; then a decision about what to recommend; then a decision to accept the recommendation or not; then a decision to implement the recommendation; then various offices deciding how they will implement the change; and so on. Each round becomes an opportunity to build support or block—overtly or covertly—further action. A strategic political actor needs to cultivate support at every decision round.

4. **Required degree of agreement.** This factor considers how many actors or offices must agree on some action or organizational change in order to proceed. Can one person or one office say *This is it, go do it!* or must a coalition of key actors and offices agree? This factor is related to decision arenas and decision rounds because the required degree of agreement may change from setting to setting (e.g., majority vote in the board, consensus in the executive committee, the boss's decision in a particular office). Because it impacts decision-making time and effort as well as the distribution of power, balancing the degree of agreement between dictatorial and consensus extremes will be a key political choice—and subject to both overt and covert forces.

5. **Access to information.** This factor considers who has access to what information related to a particular decision or change initiative. Those who possess more or better information can exercise greater power in decision-making. For better or worse, strategic political actors in organizations will attempt to manage information to their advantage by sharing more or less. While broad-based sharing of information may be needed to gain support and advance a change initiative, those opposed to the change may seek to limit the sharing as a way subtly or covertly to undermine the effort.

6. **Reciprocity.** This factor considers whether reciprocity is expected in organizational decision-making, and if so, in what ways it happens. *Reciprocity* is the exchange of favors or compensation

for giving up something of value. The favors or compensation can include friendly gestures and cooperative attitudes in return for supporting a decision. A manager who agrees to outsourcing may be "compensated" by a favorable reassignment. Often there are implicit or hidden reciprocity expectations related to organizational changes. If these are not met there could be hidden resistance or an absence of support.

7. **Expected styles.** These are the very broad norms that prescribe the acceptable behaviors in a particular organization's decision-making process. Are people supposed to be loud, aggressive, and strong-willed? Should they present their case orally or in writing? Will the presentation of personal feelings strengthen or weaken their case? Should they lobby out in front or behind the scenes? Strategic political actors will attempt to match their style to the expectations of the organization. To do otherwise may risk mismatches that lead to no-go decisions.

8. **Types of sanctions.** This factor considers whether violations of the organization's political norms are policed and punished. Can actors deviate from expected behaviors without negative sanctions? What happens if the norm of reciprocity is ignored? What happens when information is shared when it should not be, or information is guarded that should be shared?

Effective action to advance change initiatives requires understanding an organization's political system. Change efforts that don't take account of the existing political system or are incongruent with existing political norms will run into open or covert opposition. Leading effective change requires the ability to make a solid case for change and to deal effectively with an organization's political dimension.

Diagnostic Exercise

To practice thinking politically about organizational change, here are two change scenarios. Each addresses the same change but in organizations with different political systems. The scenarios are organized to illustrate the eight factors in action. Some basic questions about that organization's political system are raised following each scenario. These questions are designed to stimulate you to begin thinking about organizational change in politically strategic ways. Finally, we compare the implications of the two political systems.

Scenario 1, ABC Corporation

Initiate an organization-wide executive development program to increase strategic thinking in the ABC Corporation.

Decision arenas. The executive committee of ABC has sole authority and responsibility for approving management and organization initiatives.

Degree of participation. The executive committee is chaired by the CEO and includes the vice presidents of finance, HRD, R&D, marketing and sales, and operations. In addition, the executive assistant to the CEO serves as the non-voting executive secretary of the committee and is responsible for all staff work in support of the committee's activities.

Decision rounds. After discussion and decision in the executive committee, approved initiatives are sent to the appropriate vice president for action and implementation. In this instance the appropriate person is the vice president of HRD. Initiatives are to be carried out within the existing budgets of the assigned vice president, unless the cost estimate is greater than $2 million per annum. When greater than $2 million, a special initiatives budget is established by the executive committee and turned over to the full and total control of the assigned vice president. The executive committee reviews progress, but not budgets, and becomes involved with expenditures only if a significant increase in the approved budget is requested after implementation has begun.

Required degree of agreement. The executive committee operates under a formal majority vote procedure. The chair (the CEO, or vice president of finance when the CEO is absent) has the authority to break ties. Informally, the CEO is viewed as having the "most important" vote, but the committee can and has overruled the CEO on a number of issues. It is, however, rare for the committee to seriously challenge a strongly held position of the CEO. Votes are taken verbally after discussion of the issues and positions of those present.

(continues)

(continued)

The executive secretary participates in the discussions but may not vote. The executive secretary, as principal staff to the committee, has a great deal of influence over what actions come before the committee, at what time, and in what format. Outside staff are sometimes invited to meetings to give presentations, but usually leave before discussion and decision.

Access to information. Typically, there is very little sharing of information among the top executives of ABC. *Knowledge is power* and *Defer to the experts* are frequently heard remarks, and most executives are guarded in what they share with others, especially outside executive committee meetings. Briefing sheets and reports are distributed by the executive secretary at, or just before, meetings.

Reciprocity. In making decisions, executives at ABC are expected to do what is right for the organization, regardless of personal impact on them or their area of responsibility. Extra efforts or sacrifices are viewed as simply doing your job and IOUs are rarely, if ever, given or demanded.

Expected styles. Presentations in executive committee meetings follow a virtually identical format established by the executive secretary in order to facilitate the efficiency and productivity of the committee. Rational arguments and analyses are presented in a concise fashion. Brief discussions of the key issues are followed by formal voice vote. The quality of staff work in preparing the briefing often has an important impact on the outcomes. Briefings are usually prepared by assorted staff and junior managers, but always presented by one of the committee members or the executive secretary.

Types of sanctions. The rules and norms of the executive committee, and, for that matter, ABC, are clear and widely known. Executives, including committee members, who do not follow the norms of the organization are left out of things. Lower-level managers are often selected out ("not executive timber") if they don't follow the norms. Topics for discussion in executive committee meetings will not be placed on the agenda unless they follow the procedures established by the executive secretary, who controls such matters.

Questions. How would you go about ensuring that an executive development program is initiated in ABC? What political considerations will be most important? How might you modify or augment your usual way of handling things to account for the political dimension of change in this scenario?

Scenario 2, XYZ Corporation

Initiate an organization-wide executive development program to increase strategic thinking in the XYZ Corporation.

Decision arenas. The management committee, executive leadership and development committee, and strategic initiatives committee of XYZ all have areas of responsibility that could include initiating an executive development program to increase strategic thinking. In addition, the CEO, supported by an executive assistant, must officially approve any initiative involving special funding over $2 million per annum. The management committee is chaired by the CEO and includes the vice presidents of finance, HRD, R&D, marketing and sales, and operations.

Degree of participation. The executive leadership and development committee is chaired by the vice president of HRD and includes the vice president of operations, director of leadership development, and two line managers. The strategic initiatives committee is chaired by the vice president of finance and includes the vice president of R&D, director of corporate strategy, and two line managers.

Decision rounds. After approval of any initiative by any of the committees, the initiative is forwarded to the CEO's executive assistant, who reviews the proposal and either returns it for further staff work or forwards it to the CEO. If the CEO approves, it is then sent to the appropriate vice president for action. In this case it is not entirely clear who the appropriate vice president is, although the likely candidate is the vice president of HRD. Approval of expenditures, however, is subject to quarterly reviews by the vice president of finance, who has the authority to stop spending if a project seems "out-of-line."

Required degree of agreement. Each committee operates by consensus. No initiative can be implemented without the formal approval of the CEO. In practice, the executive assistant can delay, block, or facilitate an initiative. Full implementation of an executive development change effort will also require the support of the vice presidents of finance and HRD, and the directors of corporate strategy and leadership development. Jurisdictional squabbles between committees have been known to tie up issues almost indefinitely.

(continues)

(continued)

Access to information. Typically, there is a lot of sharing of information and few secrets among the top executives of XYZ. Information is officially provided in advance of meetings in the form of briefing reports, and informal discussions in advance of meetings are encouraged.

Reciprocity. In making decisions, executives of XYZ are expected to do what is right for the organization, regardless of personal impact on them or their area of responsibility. Extra efforts or sacrifices are noticed, however, and executives and managers routinely exchange informal favors. A common expression is *I owe you one.*

Expected styles. A wide variety of presentation formats (formal, informal, oral, written, PowerPoint, flip chart) are used in committee meetings and elsewhere in XYZ. All seem to be effective. Rational arguments are the preferred presentation style, but appeals to emotions and ideals also work well on some occasions. "Lobbying" before, during, and after meetings is a common and accepted practice in XYZ.

Types of sanctions. A wide range of decision-making behaviors is tolerated in XYZ. While it is not exactly "no holds barred," there are few clearcut rules to follow. Sometimes dramatic actions will win the day. A favorite story in XYZ is about how the vice president of finance once secured an important decision by jumping on a chair and offering to arm wrestle anyone who disagreed. Since the vice president of finance was 5 feet, 3 inches tall and weighed about 120 pounds, everyone knew how seriously the issue was considered to be.

Questions. How would you go about ensuring that an executive development program is initiated in XYZ? What political considerations would be most important? How might you modify or augment your usual way of handling things to account for the political dimension of change in this scenario?

Answering the Reflection Questions

Let's look briefly now at some answers to the reflection questions about the ABC and XYZ political systems. The main features of each are summarized in the accompanying table.

Summary of ABC and XYZ Political Systems

Factor	ABC Corporation	XYZ Corporation
Arenas	Executive committee	Management, leadership, strategic committees
Participation	CEO, 5 VPs, non-voting executive assistant	CEO, 5 VPs, 2 directors, 4 line managers, non-voting executive assistant
Rounds	Executive committee decides; delegates with full authority up to $2M to a VP.	Approval by a committee, review by executive assistant, CEO approval, VP of finance has oversight.
Agreement	Majority vote of executive committee. Chair breaks ties. CEO has "extra weight."	Committee consensus. CEO approval. Review by executive assistant. Related committee chair concurrence.
Information	Information closely held. Little information in advance of meetings.	Information widely shared. Information provided in advance of meetings.
Reciprocity	Reciprocity not expected.	Some reciprocity expected.
Styles	Prescribed styles, rationality, brevity, high-quality briefings. No lobbying.	Wide range of styles. Appeals to emotions and inspirations acceptable. Lobbying acceptable.
Sanctions	Enforced sanctions. Must follow format and procedures set by executive assistant.	No clearcut rules or norms enforced. Wide range of styles and behaviors tolerated.

The ABC Corporation's political system is primarily defined by a reliance on formal roles and processes centered in the executive committee. The five VPs have considerable autonomy once work has been delegated to them, especially if costs of new initiatives are kept under $2 million. Influencing a decision in the executive committee depends on two factors. One is how clearly and concisely you present your argument. The second is following the procedures and processes established by the executive secretary, who is also the CEO's executive assistant. There is little information sharing and no expectations of reciprocity. We may safely infer that because the VPs are used to operating mostly autonomously they would consider requests for information from other VPs as unwanted intrusions.

Based on this quick analysis, you need to focus on several things to ensure that an executive development program is successfully initiated. Your primary focus will be to gain a favorable decision in the executive committee. Developing and presenting an excellent proposal that follows all the procedures, formats, and styles of the executive committee is essential. You will also want to establish and maintain good rapport with the CEO as well as the executive assistant/executive secretary because of the powerful gatekeeping role of that position.

In most cases, you will need only three other voting members of the executive committee to agree with your proposal, so keeping everyone happy is not essential. Given the strong delegation and autonomy norms, other VPs might be predisposed to go along with your proposal, especially if it was under $2 million and in your area of responsibility. Generally speaking, you will also want to stay on good terms with the other VPs by not asking for information about, or inquiring into, their areas of responsibility.

The XYZ Corporation's political system is more diffuse than ABC's, and requires more attention to relationships than to roles and rules. More overlapping committees and thus more people are involved in any decision. Decisions must go through several approval steps before they are ready to be implemented. Furthermore, no matter what the decision or who it is assigned to, the VP of finance can always raise questions later based on financial considerations. The norms of consensus, information sharing, and reciprocity will require more attention to relationship building than to developing a clear proposal or following established procedures.

In the XYZ Corporation, getting an executive development program initiated will require a range of considerations. Chief among these is building and maintaining good working relationships with all the actors whose support you will need. Doing things to build up credits and IOUs will help to secure favorable consideration of your proposal. This includes sharing information broadly, both as a way to help others and as a sign of good faith. Deciding which committee is most likely to approve your proposal is a major strategic choice. When doing so, you need to remember that the VP of finance, who is also the chair of the strategic initiatives committee, can raise jurisdictional questions that could slow or stop your proposal. The VP of finance will also be in a position down the road to review the implementation of your proposal from a financial perspective. Consequently, establishing a good working relationship with the VP of finance—and perhaps working jurisdictional matters out in advance—will also be essential. In presenting your proposal, you might consider using your personal power or a flair for the dramatic to help influence the decision.

The differences in the political systems of ABC and XYZ Corporations suggest that different strategies will be needed in each to successfully ensure that an executive development program is initiated. Most important, what might work well in one could lead to failure in the other.

Conclusion

The ABC and XYZ discussion demonstrates why attempting any type of organizational initiative without taking into account the political dimensions will run into hidden barriers and reduce your effectiveness. Exactly what to do and how to do it will depend, as the scenarios show, on the political system of the organization in question. You need to incorporate into your prism of beliefs about organizational change the explicit orientation that organizations are both rational-logical instruments and political systems. Effective change leadership requires political as well as managerial acumen.

CHAPTER 10

▶ # Managing Covert Processes

This book has made the case that all significant organizational change involves the dimensions of reasons, politics, inspirations, emotions, mindsets, and psychodynamics. It also suggests that, with the exception of reasons, these dimensions involve covert processes that can adversely impact a change initiative. We have explored ways to think about these covert dynamics: why they exist, their various manifestations, how to develop hunches about their presence or absence, and how to address them. This chapter offers a brief summary and some concluding thoughts as guidance to those who wish to address covert processes in their organization.

A Brief Summary

According to the Covert Processes Model, the three primary reasons something remains covert are:

- It is being denied or unexpressed because the prism of the focal system defines it as unacceptable to put on-the-table; for example, politics, inspirations, and emotions are sometimes hidden or not openly expressed.

- It involves an out-of-awareness belief or mindset in the focal system's prism that is a blind spot or filter.

- It is in the focal system's unconscious in the form of repressed or untapped psychodynamics.

The major steps for addressing covert processes include:

1. Develop hunches about covert processes by noticing what is missing, both literally and symbolically. A clue that something is missing is when there is an overemphasis or an omission in an expected pattern.

2. Check your orientation. You need to:
   - Create a safe environment.
   - Be selective and seek movement, not exposure.
   - Assume people are trying their best.
   - Look in the mirror.
   - Act consistent with expectations of you and your role.

3. Act by taking steps to:
   - Establish legitimacy.
   - Create enabling conditions.
   - Be strategic.
   - Be subtle, sometimes.

4. Address limiting beliefs in the prism through:
   - Recognizing
   - Rethinking
   - Reframing

5. Remember organizations are both rational and political systems.

Concluding Thoughts

The following are some concluding thoughts to help guide your actions.

It's about accounting for, not eliminating, covert processes. One way to think about the covert dimensions of politics, inspirations, emotions, mindsets, and psychodynamics is that they are non-rational forces that get in the way of implementing a change initiative. Ideally, they would not exist or they would be eliminated from the situation. This is an aspect of the idealized rational-logical organization that has been questioned throughout this book.

Assume covert dimensions will always exist in all organizations and all change initiatives. Your task is to account for all of their combined influences. In other words, you need to make a case for change, build political support, inspire your people, acknowledge and deal with emotions as they come up, help people recognize-rethink-reframe their mindsets to better support the change, and understand that sometimes unconscious defenses emerge in reaction to the anxieties associated with the change.

This is a lot to consider. You may need to modify the case for change to help secure better alignment among all the dimensions. Accounting for, not trying to eliminate, covert processes offers the most likely path to successful change in organizations.

Address covert processes only when needed, and always seek to empower. Although this may be an unwelcome thought, it is helpful to remember that covert processes are always present. The fact that they exist does not automatically mean that all covert processes in a focal system need to be made overt and addressed. Covert processes should be addressed only to the degree that they are blocking effectiveness, desired performance, or movement in new directions.

The decision to address a covert dynamic should always be made with the intention of empowering the focal system and its members in order to enhance their performance and effectiveness. The purpose is *never* to expose, reveal, or unveil the covert process as an end in itself. If the focal system is already achieving its desired performance, then addressing one of the many things not on-the-table may neither be needed nor appropriate.

Exercise choice in what you address. It is possible for a focal system to be effective without making all of its covert processes overt. Some covert processes will always be present. Only so much can be on-the-table at any time. Holding one set of beliefs in our prisms enables us to see some things better but also blinds us to others. Keep in mind that a covert process may be serving a positive purpose for the focal system by protecting against a perceived lack of safety in the situation. Your challenge is to create a context safe enough for people to raise and address the covert issues that seem to be most directly related to negatively impacting performance. Yes, a tall order and a useful caution.

Be clear about your purposes, principles, philosophy, and power. Ensuring your own clarity is a critical aspect of dealing with hidden dimensions effectively and a way to guard against having your own covert processes bias your thoughts and actions. First, you need clarity about your purpose. What are the intended outcomes you seek to realize? Second, clarity about your principles, in the form of the theories, values, and ethics you are applying to the specific situation. What are the ways to think and behave in the situation that are most relevant and effective? What are the core values and ethics that guide what you are willing and able to do?

Next you need clarity on your philosophy about your role vis à vis organizational change. What are your beliefs about how change occurs and what is most important for you to do in a specific situation? Finally, there is clarity about your personal and positional power and influence. What are the aspects of how you use your power and influence that are your strengths and how do you attend to those that are less potent? What are your thoughts and feelings about using your power to foster change?

Dealing with covert processes will be easier the clearer you are about your purpose, principles, philosophy, and power. In dealing with covert processes it is easy to get thrown off balance. When that happens, re-check your clarity. Everything else comes from that.

Practice multi-level, multi-dimensional, multi-modal seeing and doing. This way of working is complex and is an orientation to aspire to in your work. Put simply, it invites you to see and do—or diagnose and act—in multiple ways. Those ways include seeing and doing at individual, interpersonal, group, organization, and broader environment levels. Multi-level seeing and doing can be especially useful when working with a focal system that tends to stay focused on one level alone. As a rule of practice you might consider always looking "one level up" and "one level down" no matter what the situation. If the issue or covert dynamic is at the group level, consider how some aspect of the organization is impacting the group, as well as the way individual dynamics may be influencing team dynamics.

Multi-dimensional seeing and doing involves actively considering how the six different dimensions of reasons, politics, inspirations, emotions, mindsets, and psychodynamics are simultaneously impacting a situation. Each is a potential source or solution for whatever covert difficulty may be at issue. Finally, multi-modal seeing and doing assumes that both literal and symbolic communications are important sources of information about what may be happening covertly. People may tell you directly that there is a lack of an effective vision to guide the change effort. The lack can also be revealed through a symbolic expression: *We seem to be operating in the dark. We don't know where we are going.*

Track patterns to discern what is core. Along with multi-level, multi-dimensional, multi-modal seeing and doing goes tracking. Tracking refers to the ability to discern what is core to a situation by noting any recurring patterns or themes being expressed by the focal system. It also involves noting any omissions or overemphases in the patterns. You track what is being expressed in multiple ways, in multiple places, at multiple times. The ability to see core themes and patterns that might be covert will allow you to impact the focal system most effectively.

In one meeting a group of executives created a comprehensive change strategy but did not include a change vision statement. In another meeting middle managers talked about *operating in the dark, not being able to really see where we are going,* and *lacking foresight.* A version of the corporate logo showing a figure with its eyes shut was noticed in the marketing department. The absence of vision stood out if you were able to track what was being expressed literally and symbolically in many different parts of the organization. One of the core issues impeding that organization may have been the "vision thing," even if this was not being openly discussed or addressed.

Think politically. Thinking politically means looking at organizations as political systems involving power and then acting accordingly. It also means acknowledging that you sometimes need to be a political actor. Whether you are a leader, staff specialist, or consultant, you need to act in ways that impact the existing power system in order to achieve desired outcomes. Key aspects of this orientation include knowing who the stakeholders and political players are and anticipating their mindsets, interests, and potential agendas. It also means understanding the focal system's political dynamics. Finally, it means using your personal and positional power to be an agent of change. This is an orientation that accepts power and political processes as inherent aspects of organizations and therefore of effective organizational change.

Find, form, and frame reality. This is an alliterative way to remind you that the beliefs and assumptions in a focal system's prism interpret the world and create the meanings that guide its behavior and responses. In that sense, the meanings created by our prisms create our reality. Yes, there are objective empirical events, but it is the meanings given to those events by the focal system's prism that creates its reality. Recognizing, rethinking, and reframing, which are ways to find, form, and frame reality, become core ways to change a focal system by impacting how its prism interprets the world. Finding, forming, and framing reality, when successful, are powerful ways to address covert processes. In order to do so effectively, however, you need to be guided by a desire to create alignment, seek empowerment not embarrassment, exercise choice about what to do and when to do it, ensure your own clarity, practice multi-level/ dimensional/modal seeing and doing, track patterns, and think politically. Otherwise you will not be able to find the focal system's current reality, nor have enough purposeful intent and power to help form or frame a new reality.

Ethics, ethics, ethics. Because covert processes include unconscious and out-of-awareness dynamics, or involve psychological safety issues, ethical considerations are very important. These have been raised throughout the book but are repeated here for emphasis:

- Covert processes don't always need to be addressed, and the conditions to properly address them can't always be established.

- Addressing covert processes is always done for the purpose of providing more choice and empowerment to a focal system.

- Ensuring enough safety is always your principle concern, and you must always remember that safety is in the eye of the beholder.

- Do things that are within your growing edge of competence and leave other things alone, or refer to others with greater skills or experience as appropriate.

- If your attempts to create a safe and enabling context to put things on-the-table are not successful, don't force the issue. The covert dynamic may be deeper and more complex than you think.

- Continue to learn and develop your skills in order to increase your ability to effectively and ethically address covert dynamics.

Conclusion

You will be more effective in developing and implementing change when you are able to help individuals, groups, and organizations give voice to their secret hopes and fears, create ways to explore previously untested or unimagined possibilities, and develop enough safety and confidence to engage previously unsafe topics. All this and more will be needed to accomplish the breakthrough changes required for success in today's complex and ever-evolving world.

Bibliography of Selected Topics

Double-loop Learning and Defensive Routines

Argyris, Chris. "Double Loop Learning." *Harvard Business Review.* 55 (5) (1977): 115–125.

Argyris, Chris. *Reasoning, Learning and Action.* San Francisco: Jossey-Bass, 1982.

Argyris, Chris. *Overcoming Organizational Defenses.* Boston: Allyn & Bacon, 1990.

Argyris, Chris. *Knowledge for Action.* San Francisco: Jossey-Bass, 1993.

Argyris, Chris and Schön, Donald A. *Theory in Practice.* San Francisco: Jossey-Bass, 1974.

Argyris, Chris and Schön, Donald A. *Organizational Learning: A Theory of Action Perspective.* Reading, Mass: Addison Wesley, 1978.

Freedman, Arthur M. "The Undiscussable Sides of Implementing Transformational Change." *Consulting Psychology Journal: Practice and Research,* 49 (1) (1997): 51–76.

Schön, Donald A. *The Reflective Practitioner.* New York: Basic Books, 1983.

Fear and Emotion in the Workplace

Berman Brown, Reva B. "Emotions in Organizations: The Case of English University Business School Academics." *Journal of Applied Behavioral Science,* 33 (2) (1997): 247–262.

Fineman, Stephen.(Ed.) *Emotion in Organizations*. London: Sage Publications, 1993.

Goleman, Daniel. *Emotional Intelligence*. New York: Bantam Books, 1995.

Kasl, Elizabeth, Marsick, Victoria J., and Dechant, Kathleen. "Teams as Learners: A Research-Based Model of Team Learning." *Journal of Applied Behavioral Science*, 33 (2) (1997): 227–246.

Kotter, John P., and Cohen, Dan S. *The Heart of Change*. Boston: Harvard Business School Press, 2002.

Mulvey, Paul W., Veiga, John F., and Elsass, Priscilla M. "When Teammates Raise a White Flag." *Academy of Management Executive*, 10 (1)(1996): 40–49.

Plas, Jeanne M., and Hoover-Dempsey, Kathleen V. *Working up a Storm: Anger, Anxiety, Joy and Fears on the Job – and How to Handle Them*. New York: W. W. Norton & Company, 1988.

Ryan, Kathleen D., and Ostreich, Daniel K. *Driving Fear Out of the Workplace: Creating the High-Trust, High Performance Organization*. San Francisco: Jossey-Bass, 1998.

Stone, Douglas, Patton, Bruce and Heen, Sheila. *Difficult Conversations: How to Discuss What Matters Most*. New York: Penguin Books, 1999.

Power and Politics in Organizations

Bacharach, Samuel B., and Lawler, Edward J. *Power and Politics in Organizations*. San Francisco: Jossey-Bass, 1980.

Greiner, Larry E., and Schein, Virginia E. *Power and Organization Development: Mobilizing Power to Implement Change*. Reading, MA: Addison-Wesley, 1988.

Kotter, John P. *Power and Influence: Beyond Formal Authority*. New York: Free Press, 1985.

Marshak, Robert J. "Politics, Public Organizations, and OD." *OD Practitioner*, 24 (4) (1992): 5–8.

Pfeiffer, Jeffrey. *Power in Organizations*. Marshfield, MA: Pittman, 1981.

Pfeffer, Jeffrey. *Managing with Power: Politics and Influence in Organizations*. Boston: Harvard Business School Press, 1992.

Weber, Max. *From Max Weber*, H. Gerth and C. W. Mills (Eds.). New York: Oxford University Press, 1946.

The Prism and its Contents

Beck, Aaron T. *Cognitive Therapy*. New York: New American Library, 1976.

Bennett, Hal Z. *The Lens of Perception*. Berkely, CA: Celestial Arts, 1987

Cameron, Kim S., and Quinn, Robert E. *Diagnosing and Changing Organizational Culture*, Reading, MA: Addison-Wesley, 1999.

Dodson-Gray, Elizabeth. *Patriarchy as a Conceptual Trap*. Wellesley, MA: Roundtable Press, 1982.

Ellis, Albert. *Reason and Emotion in Psychotherapy*. New York: Lyle Stuart, 1962.

Kuhn, Thomas S. *The Structure of Scientific Revolutions, 2nd edition*. Chicago: University of Chicago Press, 1970.

Langer, Ellen J. *Mindfulness*. Reading, MA: Addison-Wesley, 1989.

Lipson, Abigal, and Perkins, David N. *Block: Getting Out of Your Own Way*. New York: Carol Publishing Group, 1990.

Pepper, Stephen C. *World Hypotheses: A Study in Evidence*. Berkeley, CA: University of California Press. 1961.

Schein, Edgar H. *Organization Culture and Leadership*, 3rd Edition. New York: Wiley, 2004.

Process Consultation

Schein, Edgar H. *Process Consultation*, Vol. II. Reading, MA: Addison-Wesley, 1987.

Schein, Edgar H. *Process Consultation*, Vol. I, 2nd Edition. Reading, MA: Addison-Wesley, 1988.

Schein, Edgar H. *Process Consultation Revisited: Building the Helping Relationship*. Reading, MA: Addison-Wesley, 1999.

Psychodynamics in the Workplace

Czander, William M. *The Psychodynamics of Work and Organizations: Theory and Application*. New York: Guilford Press, 1993.

De Board, Robert. *The Psychoanalysis of Organizations: A Psychoanalytic Approach to Behavior in Groups and Organizations*. London: Routledge, 1978.

Hirschhorn, Larry. *The Workplace Within: Psychodynamics of Organizational Life*. Cambridge, MA: MIT Press, 1991.

Kets de Vries, Manfried F. R. *Organizations on the Couch: Handbook of Psychoanalysis and Management*. San Francisco: Jossey-Bass, 1991.

Menzies, Isabel E. P. *The Functioning of Social Systems as a Defense Against Anxiety*. London: The Tavistock Institute of Human Relations, 1993.

Obholzer, Anton, and Roberts, Vega Z. *The Unconscious at Work*. London: Routledge, 1994.

Segal, Morely. *Points of Influence: A Guide to Using Personality Theory at Work*. San Francisco: Jossey-Bass, 1997.

Psychosynthesis

Assagioli, Roberto. *The Act of Will*. New York: Penguin Books, 1974.

Assagioli, Roberto. *Psychosynthesis*. New York: Penguin Books, 1976.

Ferruci, Piero. *What We May Be*. Los Angeles: J. P. Tarcher, 1982.

Hardy, Jean. *A Psychology with a Soul: Psychosynthesis in Evolutionary Context*. London: Routledge & Kegan Paul, 1987.

Rational and Non-Rational Perspectives on Organizations

Bolman, Lee G., and Deal, Terrence E. *Reframing Organizations,* Second Edition. San Francisco: Jossey-Bass, 1997.

Egan, Gerard. *Working the Shadow Side*. San Francisco: Jossey-Bass, 1994.

Morgan, Gareth. *Images of Organization,* Second Edition. Thousand Oaks, CA: Sage, 1997.

Reframing and Sensemaking

Bandler, Richard and Grinder, John. *Reframing: NLP and the Transformation of Meaning*. Moab, Utah: Real People Press, 1982.

Bartunek, Jean M. "Changing Interpretive Schemas and Organizational Restructuring: The Example of a Religious Order." *Administrative Science Quarterly*, 29, 355–372. 1984.

Daft, Richard L., and Weick, Karl E. "Towards a Model of Organizations as Interpretive Systems." *Academy of Management Review*, 9 (2), 284–295, 1984.

Fairhurst, Gail T. and Sarr, Robert A. *The Art of Framing: Managing the Language of Leadership.* San Francisco: Jossey-Bass Publishers, 1996.
Goffman, Erving. *Frame Analysis.* New York: Harper and Row, 1974.
Lakoff, George. *Don't Think of an Elephant: Know Your Values and Frame the Debate.* White River Junction, VT: Chelsea Publishing, 2004.
Weick, Karl E. *Sensemaking in Organizations.* Thousand Oaks, CA: Sage, 1995.
Weick, Karl E. *The Social Psychology of Organizing,* Second Edition. New York: McGraw Hill, 1979.

Symbolic Diagnosis

Donnellon, Anne. *Team Talk: The Power of Language in Team Dynamics.* Boston: Harvard Business School Press, 1996.
Fontana, David. *The Secret Language of Symbols: A Visual Guide to Symbols and Their Meanings.* San Francisco: Chronicle Books, 1993.
Furth, Gregg M. *The Secret World of Drawings: Healing Through Art.* Boston: Sigo Press, 1988.
Lakoff, George, and Johnson, Mark. *Metaphors We Live By,* Second Edition. Chicago, University of Chicago Press, 2003.
Marshak, Robert J. "Managing the Metaphors of Change." *Organizational Dynamics,* 22 (1) (1993): 44–56.
Marshak, Robert. J., and Katz, Judith H. "The Symbolic Side of OD." *OD Practitioner,* 24 (2) (1992): 1–5.

Tavistock Group Relations Approach

Banet, Anthoney G., and Hayden, Charla. "A Tavistock Primer." *The 1977 Annual Handbook for Group Facilitators.* San Diego, CA: University Associates, p. 155–167, 1977.
Bion, Wilfred R. *Experiences in Groups.* New York: Basic Books, 1959.
Colman, Arthur D., and Bexton, Harold (Eds.) *Group Relations Reader 1,* Washington, DC: A. K. Rice Institute, 1975.
Colman, Arthur D., and Geller, Marvin H. (Eds.). *Group Relations Reader 2,* Washington, DC: A. K. Rice Institute, 1985.
Rice, A. Kenneth. *Learning for Leadership: Interpersonal and Intergroup Relations.* London: Tavistock Publications, 1965.

Rioch, Margaret O. "The Work of Wilfred R. Bion on Groups." *Psychiatry*, 33, p. 56–66, 1970.

References

Argyris, Chris. "Double Loop Learning." *Harvard Business Review,* 55 (5) (1977): 115–125.

Argyris, Chris, and Schön, Donald A. *Theory in Practice*. San Francisco: Jossey-Bass, 1974.

Banet, Anthoney G., and Hayden, Charla. "A Tavistock Primer." *The 1977 Annual Handbook for Group Facilitators*. San Diego, CA: University Associates, p. 155–167, 1977.

Egan, Gerard. *Working the Shadow Side*. San Francisco: Jossey-Bass, 1994.

Ferruci, Piero. *What We May Be*. Los Angeles: J. P. Tarcher, 1982.

Ellis, Albert. *Reason and Emotion in Psychotherapy*. New York: Lyle Stuart, 1962.

Festinger, Leon. *A Theory of Cognitive Dissonance*. Palo Alto, CA: Stanford University Press, 1957.

Ghoshal, Sumantra. "Bad Management Theories are Destroying Good Management Practices." *Academy of Management Learning and Education,* 4 (1) (2005): 75–91.

Goffman, Erving. *Frame Analysis*. New York: Harper and Row, 1974.

Greiner, Larry E., and Schein, Virginia E. *Power and Organization Development: Mobilizing Power to Implement Change*. Reading, MA: Addison-Wesley, 1988.

Kotter, John P., and Cohen, Dan S. *The Heart of Change*. Boston: Harvard Business School Press, 2002.

Kübler-Ross, Elizabeth. *On Death and Dying.* New York: Macmillan 1973.

Marshak, Robert J., and Katz, Judith H. "Diagnosing Covert Processes in Groups and Organizations." *OD Practitioner*, 29 (1) (1997): 33–42.

Marshak, Robert J., and Katz, Judith H. "Keys to Unlocking Covert Processes: How to Recognize and Address the Hidden Dimensions of Individuals, Groups and Organizations." *OD Practitioner*, 33 (2) (2001): 3–10.

Marshak, Robert J. "Claiming your Power and Leadership as an OD Consultant." *OD Practitioner*, 33 (4) (2001): 35–40.

Marshak, Robert J. "Generative Conversations: How to Use Deep Listening and Transforming Talk in Coaching and Consulting." *OD Practitioner*, 36 (3) (2004): 25–29.

Ostrom, Elinor. "Strategy and Structure of Interdependent Decision-making Mechanisms." *Workshop in Political Theory and Policy Analysis*, Indiana University, Bloomington, IN Series: Workshop Working Paper, W67–3, 1967.

Schein, Edgar H. *Process Consultation Revisited: Building the Helping Relationship.* Reading, MA: Addison-Wesley, 1999.

Senge, Peter M. *The Fifth Discipline.* New York: Doubleday, 1990.

Tuckman, Bruce W. "Development Sequence in Small Groups. *Psychological Bulletin*, 63 (1965): 284–399.

Weber, Max. *From Max Weber*, H. Gerth and C. W. Mills (Eds.). New York: Oxford University Press, 1946.

Index

ABC Corporation, diagnostic exercise, 155–156
abilities, untapped, 51
above-the-clouds
  secret hopes and wishes, 28
  work group agendas, 48–49
acceptance, executive, 32
accusations, avoiding, 94–95
achievements, progress reports on, 131–132
acknowledgement, giving desired, 131–132
action, reframing for more productive, 129–130
actions, responses to diagnostic questions, 110–111
agendas
  hidden, xi, 26–30
  personal, 28
  sanctioning topics by, 89
  work group, 48
agents, change, 2–3
agreement, required degree of, 153
Alpha Corporation, 42–46
Analyteks, Inc., 3–7
answers, feasible vs. right, 147
arenas, decision, 152
Argyris, Chris, double-loop learning, 12–13, 115–116
Assagioli, Roberto, psychosynthesis, 29
assumptions
  basic, 76–77
  changing to reflect present situation, 117–118
  implementing change, 165
  reframing implicit, 128
  tacit, xi, 26–27
  unexamined, 12

attributes
  unacceptable, 29
  unconscious positive, 29–30

behavior
  acceptable, 26
  modeling unblocked, 99
  new, 134
  patterns of, 36
  value driven, 117–118
belief system, visiting or importing a new, 121–122
beliefs
  adjusting to present situation, 117–118
  challenging, 111, 116–119, 121
  confronting, 105
  limiting, 89
biases, avoiding personal, 73
blind spots, xi
  organizational, 92
brutality, truth, 55

case studies
  Alpha Corporation, 42–46
  Analyteks, Inc., 3–7
  Comfort Foods, 81–84
  Global Solutions, 140–142
  HRD consultant, 137–140
  InfoTech Division, 111–113
  Smith-Jones Corporation, 63–66
  U.S. Department of Agriculture, 100–102
  Whiz Tech Corporation, 30–31
censorship, bypassing conscious, 54
centrality, addressing core beliefs, 96
change
  dimensions of, 5
  name, 10–11
  organizational, xi

charts, organization, 60
checklist, organizational change,
  14–17
childhood, lessons learned in, 22–23
clarity, ensuring, 166
clouds. *See* above-the-clouds
clue, covert processes diagnostic
  formula, 37
coaching, reframing, 130
Cohen, Dan and John Kotter, *The
  Heart of Change*, 9
collaboration
  focusing on the focal system, 79
  promoting, 122
  symbolic reframing, 130
collusion, covert, 27
Comfort Foods, 81–84
commitment, absence of real, 34
common ground, creating, 145–146
communication
  literal, 55
  progress reports on achievements,
    131–132
  symbolic, 54–55, 61–63
  symbolic means of, 99
  The 4 M's of symbolic, 57–66
compensation, unconscious dynamics,
  50–51
competence, questioning, 70
concerns, indirect expression of, 33
conditions, enabling, 92–93
conflict, organizational structure and
  role, 78
congruence, maintaining, 122
connotation, changing from negative
  to positive, 128–129
consultation, process, xii
context
  determining, 48
  frame of reference, 38–40
  understanding, 42–46
control, establishing a sense of, 71
covert processes, defined, 1–2
Covert Processes Diagnostic Formula,
  application of the, 40–46
Covert Processes Model, Whiz Tech
  Corporation, 30–34

cultures
  challenging, 119–120
  changing organizational or societal,
    24–25
  limitations imposed by, 25
  organizational, 12
curiosity, inquiring out of, 74
Current Research Inventory System
  (CRIS), 101–102

danger, frame of reference, 72
Dealing with Covert Processes
  Workshop (Marshak and Katz),
  xii, 187
decisions, organizational politics, 149
defenses, unconscious, 165
denials
  covering up inadequacies, 39
  emotional involvement, 70
  unconscious dynamics, 50
  unconscious processes of, 4
desires, unexpressed, 28
diagnosis
  organizational framework, 152–154
  symbolic communication, 53–67
dimensions, organizational change,
  15–17
display, visual, 108
disputing, methods of, 122–123
dissonance, cognitive, 122
doing, multi-level, multi-dimensional,
  multi-modal, 166–167
double-loop learning, 12–13, 115–116
doubts, reluctance to express, 32–33
dynamics
  exploring covert, 20
  hidden, 1
  political, 7
  unconscious, xi
  work group, 46–52

economics, adjusting decisions to
  reflect current, 117–118
efforts, best, 94–95
elephant-in-the-room, xi
Ellis, Albert, methods of disputing
  beliefs, 123

emotions
  dimension of organizational change,
    16
  organizational change, 9–11
empathy, showing, 77
emphases, focal system, 39, 41
empowerment
  focal systems, 165
  reframing interventions, 130–131
environment, creating a
    psychologically safe, 69–72
error, fear of, 120–121
ethics, personal, 168–169
events, impact of prior experience on
    viewpoint, 23–24
exercises,
  diagnostic scenarios, 154–161
  napkin trick, 101–102
expectations
  acting consistent with, 79–81
  organizational change proposal, 10
  renegotiating, 80–81, 96
experience, field of, 20–22
exposure, avoiding for its own sake,
    75
expressions, symbolic, 51, 53, 56

failure, vs. feedback, 130
fear
  of error, 120–121
  overt emotionality, 10
  of repercussions, 70
  retribution, 72
  of ridicule, 28
  unconscious influence of, 28–29
  unspoken, 40
filters, prism, 49
focal systems
  context, 38–40
  defense mechanisms, 28–29
  empowerment, 165
  field of experience, 20–22
  identifying, 32
  mandating exploration of issues,
    88–89
  seeking change, 34
focus, keeping your, 77–79

forces
  eliminating non-rational, 164–165
  hidden, xii
formula, covert processes diagnostic,
    36–37, 40–46
four major modalities (The 4 M's),
    56–66
frame, understanding another's,
    131–132
framework, diagnostic organizational,
    152–154
framing, issues for consideration,
    93–94

Gestalt psychology, 35–36
Global Solutions, 140–142
gotcha!, playing, 67
group development, stages of small,
    38

help, coded signals for, 80–81
honesty, truth, 55
hopes, secret wishes and, xi
hunches
  better, 42–46
  developing, 35, 76–77

image, protecting a positive, 136
images, word, 53
information, access, 153
InfoTech Division, 111–113
initiatives
  change, 2, 147
  introducing, 154–161
inquiry
  climate of, 93
  inviting further, 77
  nonjudgmental, 73–74
  psychological safety, 70–71
inspiration
  dimension of organizational change,
    15
  power of, 8–9
integration, facilitating a merger,
    81–84
intelligence, emotional, 9

intent, identifying and maintaining positive, 132–133
intentions, covert, ix
interrelationships, discovering, 108–111
interventions
  confronting beliefs, 105–106
  recognizing, 106–111
  reframing, 132–136
  reframing vs. rethinking, 127–128
  rethinking, 114–121
invitations, to explore issues, 93
issues
  framing for consideration, 93–94
  indirect expression of attitude towards, 33
  methods for addressing, 91–92
  raising, 88–92
  spontaneous, 27
  within the focal system's prism, 90

Katz, Judith H.
  "Dealing with Covert Processes Workshop", xii
  and Robert J. Marshak, Covert Processes Model, 19–34
keys, facilitating corporate change, 69–85
King, Martin Luther, "I Have a Dream", 8
Kotter, John and Dan Cohen, *The Heart of Change*, 9
Kübler-Ross, Elizabeth, organizational change, 10

language, body, 59
leadership, model for change, 14
learning, double-loop, 12–13, 115–116
legitimacy, establishing, 87–92, 107–108
lenses, focal system, 23
lessons, childhood, 22–23
limitations
  imposed by culture, 25
  tacit assumptions, 26–27

limits, focal system, 22
location, challenging focal system issues, 90–91

Marshak, Robert J. ,
  about the author, 187–188
  and Judith H. Katz, Covert Processes Model, 19–34
media
  interpreting, 62–63
  representative of a group, 59–60
  symbolic communication, 57
mental models, resistance to change, 12
merger, facilitating integration into a holding company, 81–84
messages
  coded, 80–81
  literal, 54–55
  management's mixed, 33–34
  symbolic, 54–55, 67, 99
  unspoken parts of, 6
metaphor
  interpreting, 60–61
  listening for, 57–58
  symbolic communication, 57
method
  addressing issues, 91–92
  analysis-think-change, 9
  disputing beliefs, 123
  see-feel-change, 9
mindsets
  dimension of organizational change, 16
  executive, 5
  HRD vs. Career Service vs. Political, 151
  resistance to change, 11–13
mirror, self-reflection, 77–79, 97
missing, discovering what is, 35–36
modalities, the four major (The 4 M's), 56–66
model, Covert Processes, 19–34
models, formal, 38
motivation, identifying, 94
motives, listening without questioning, 83

movement
  facilitating, 73–76
  interpreting, 62
  observing the group's, 58–59
  precipitating, 97–98
  symbolic communication, 57
music
  hearing the group's, 58
  listening to the group's, 61–62
  symbolic communication, 57

name, changing a corporate, 10–11
napkin, consolidating ideas to fit on a, 101–102
negotiations, management and union, 115–116

observations, distorted, 78–79
obstacles, overcoming, 92–93
off-the-table
  spontaneous issues, 27
  what stays, 26–30
omissions, significant, 39–41
on-the-table
  strategies for putting things, 87–103
  what goes, 25–26
  work group agendas, 48
openness, in the workplace, ix
options
  available to focal system, 132
  generating new, 132–133
organizations, as political systems, 151–158
outcomes, clarifying, 74, 132–133

paradigms
  challenging existing, 119
  shifting, 12, 24
participation, degree of, 152
patterns
  behavior, 113–114
  covert, 37–38
  historic, 43
  internal politics, 111–113
  normal, 38
  recognizing, 40–42

rethinking, 124–125
  tracking, 167
people, considering needs and interests of, 7
perspectives
  organizational, 149–151
  political, 7
  political vs. rational-logical, 146–147
  power vs. political, 147–148
philosophy, clarity of, 166
pictures, symbolic expressions, 62–63
polarities, working the, 136
political systems
  diagnostic exercises, 155–159
  summary of ABC and XYZ, 159–161
politics
  dimensions of organizational change, 15
  internal, 111–113
  organizational, xi, 148–151
  organizational behavior, 7
  overlooking, 4–5
  perspectives on, 144–147
possibilities, imagining untapped, 29
power
  change and use of, 148
  clarity, 166
  competition for, 27–28
Precision Corporation, fear of error, 120–121
preferences, avoiding personal, 73
presentations
  bullet-proof, 111–113
  indirectly addressing issues, 98
principles
  clarity of, 166
  reframing, 132–136
prism
  challenging beliefs within the, 121–123
  contents of, 23
  creating a new operational, 32
  interventions within the existing, 105–106

prism *(continued)*
  limitations imposed by, 25–30
  limitations of tacit assumptions,
    26–27
  perception of focal system, 21–22
  politics from a personal, 144–146
  safety of subject, 70–71
  stepping into the focal system's, 133
  work group frame of reference, 49
  working within a focal system's, 142
problem-solving, double-loop
    learning, 115–116
process consultation, xii
processes
  covert, 26–30
  overt, 25–26
programs, identifying a common
    structure, 100–102
projection, unconscious dynamics, 50
psychodynamics
  dimension of organizational change,
    16
  reaction to change, 13–14
  unconscious, 5
psychology, Gestalt, 35–36
psychosynthesis, 29
public agencies, administrative
    structure, 150
purpose, clarity of, 166

questions
  diagnostic, 108–110
  diagnostic exercise reflection, 158–
    161
  reframing a change intervention,
    140–142
  suppression of honest comments, 33

rationalizations, excessive, 4
readiness, addressing issues, 95
reality
  focal system and, 131, 168
  reframing, 106
reason, over-emphasis on, 3
reasons
  dimensions of organizational
    change, 15

making a case for change, 5–6
recession, value-driven behavior, 118
reciprocity, expectations of, 153–154
recognition, interventions, 106–111
reframing
  basics of, 128–132
  interventions, 106
  principles, 132–136
relationships, building trust, 116
renaming, changing perceptions by,
    134–135
renegotiating, expectations, 80–81, 96
repression, unconscious dynamics, 50
resistance, irrational, 6
responses, interpreting diagnostic
    question, 108–110
rethinking
  interventions, 106
  stimulating, 123
retribution, fear of, 72
ridicule, fear of, 28
risk, minimizing perceived, 134
rituals, establishing order and safety,
    99–100
role, renegotiating expectations,
    80–81, 96
rounds, decision making, 152–153
rules, ground, 107–108

safety
  creating an atmosphere of, 88
  establishing, 107–108
  promoting, 165
  psychological, 70–71, 85
sanctions
  anticipated, 154
  legitimization of topics, 89
scenarios, diagnostic exercises, 154–
    161
Schein, Ed, process consultation, xii
Schön, Donald, double-loop learning,
    115–116
Seashore, Edie, "Up until now",
    127–128
seating, symbolic reframing, 130
secrecy, personal agendas, 28

secrets
 family, 2
 revealing, 75–76
seeing, multi-level, multi-dimensional,
 multi-modal, 166–167
self-awareness, distorted observations,
 78–79
self-interests, differing, 3–4
sequencing, order of importance,
 95–96
setting, creating a safe, 77
signals, coded, 80–81
sinking ship, symbolic expressions, 53
situation, viewed through focal
 system, 131
Smith-Jones Corporation, 63–66
social systems, covert processes
 within, 30–31
solutions
 double-loop learning, 115–116
 seeking within an accepted structure,
 102–103
spin, vs. reframing, 129–131
statement, vision, 8–9
steps, addressing covert processes, 164
stories, indirectly addressing issues
 through, 98
strategies, putting things on-the-table,
 87–103
structure, identifying a common,
 100–102
styles, organizational expectations,
 154
subconscious, repressed and buried
 thoughts, 28–29
subtlety, addressing issues with,
 97–100
success, measuring, 75–76
superconscious, the untapped, 29–30
support, signaling, 77
symbolic communication. *See*
 communication, symbolic
symbols, establishing order and safety,
 99–100
synergies, untapped, 51
systems, organizations as political,
 151–158

table
 clearing the, 92–93
 See also off-the-table, on-the-table,
 under-the-table
task forces, creating a new corporate
 vision, 32
Tavistock, group dynamics approach,
 51
The Heart of Change (Kotter and
 Cohen), 9
theories
 challenging outdated, 118–119
 formal, 24, 38
 Tuckman's, 38, 41
thinking
 disputing ways of, 122–123
 either/or, 135–136
 mindset limitations, 12–13
 political, 167–168
thoughts,
 repressed and buried, 28–29
 systems, 24
threat
 avoidance of becoming a, 72
 protecting the focal system from, 72
 reducing, 133–134
 of repercussions, 70
timing
 challenging focal system issues, 90
 order of importance, 95–96
topics
 raising, 89–92
 that remain covert, 163–164
transference, unconscious dynamics,
 50
traps, hidden conceptual, 12
trick, napkin, 101–102
trust
 building relationships, 116
 establishing, 71
truth, telling the, 55
Tuckman's theory, 38, 41
under-the-table
 things denied, 27–28
 work group agendas, 48
understandings, role clarity, 79–80

unions, management negotiations
    with, 115–116
U.S. Department of Agriculture,
    100–102

values
  adjusting to present day economics,
    117–118
  altruistic, 28
viewpoint, impact of experience on
    interpretation of events, 23–24
vision
  implementing a new, 30–31
  new operating prism, 32
voice, group, 51

weapon, truth, 55
Whiz Tech Corporation, 30–31
wishes, secret hopes and, xi

work groups
  considering needs and interests of, 7
  dynamics, 46–52
Worksheet
  Covert Processes Model, 47
  recognizing prism patterns, 124–125
workshops, Dealing with Covert
    Processes, xii
worldviews, changing, 12

XYZ Corporation, diagnostic
    exercise, 157–158

About the Author

Bob Marshak has led a double life as a practitioner and scholar of management and organizational change. For more than thirty years he has worked as a consultant and executive with global corporations and government agencies to plan and manage change, develop new strategies and structures, challenge limiting mindsets, work cross-culturally, and build more effective teamwork. He is noted for his strategic and incisive thinking, skill at reading organizational dynamics in multi-dimensional ways, and ability to cut to the core of situations and issues. He has used these skills to help people put things "on-the-table" in board rooms, meeting rooms, and classrooms around the world. Bob is also the co-creator of the Dealing with Covert Processes Workshop, which for more than fifteen years has helped managers and consultants learn more about the hidden dimensions of individuals, groups, and organizations.

In the world of scholarship, Bob is known for cutting-edge thinking about the dynamics of organizational change. He is internationally recognized for his expertise on covert processes in organizations, as well as how to use the hidden power of language and symbolic meaning to facilitate change in organizations. He is a frequent presenter at conferences and has written more than forty articles about organizational consulting and change, including several that are considered classics in the field. Bob has worked with thousands of participants in organizational consulting and change leadership programs at universities and institutes in North America, Europe, and Asia. Most recently he was appointed scholar-in-residence for the AU/NTL Masters in Organization Development Program at the School of Public Affairs, American University, Washington, DC.

Among his many awards, he received the OD Network's Lifetime Achievement Award in recognition of his outstanding contributions to the field of organization development as a consultant, educator, and author. He has a BA from Duke University, and MPA and PhD degrees from American University.

About Berrett-Koehler Publishers

Berrett-Koehler is an independent publisher dedicated to an ambitious mission: Creating a World that Works for All.

We believe that to truly create a better world, action is needed at all levels—individual, organizational, and societal. At the individual level, our publications help people align their lives and work with their deepest values. At the organizational level, our publications promote progressive leadership and management practices, socially responsible approaches to business, and humane and effective organizations. At the societal level, our publications advance social and economic justice, shared prosperity, sustainable development, and new solutions to national and global issues.

We publish groundbreaking books focused on each of these levels. To further advance our commitment to positive change at the societal level, we have recently expanded our line of books in this area and are calling this expanded line "BK Currents."

A major theme of our publications is "Opening Up New Space." They challenge conventional thinking, introduce new points of view, and offer new alternatives for change. Their common quest is changing the underlying beliefs, mindsets, institutions, and structures that keep generating the same cycles of problems, no matter who our leaders are or what improvement programs we adopt.

We strive to practice what we preach—to operate our publishing company in line with the ideas in our books. At the core of our approach is *stewardship,* which we define as a deep sense of responsibility to administer the company for the benefit of all of our "stakeholder" groups: authors, customers, employees, investors, service providers, and the communities and environment around us. We seek to establish a partnering relationship with each stakeholder that is open, equitable, and collaborative.

We are gratified that thousands of readers, authors, and other friends of the company consider themselves to be part of the "BK Community." We hope that you, too, will join our community and connect with us through the ways described on our website at www. bkconnection.com.

Be Connected

Visit Our Website

Go to www.bkconnection.com to read exclusive previews and excerpts of new books, find detailed information on all Berrett-Koehler titles and authors, browse subject-area libraries of books, and get special discounts.

Subscribe to Our Free E-Newsletter

Be the first to hear about new publications, special discount offers, exclusive articles, news about bestsellers, and more! Get on the list for our free e-newsletter by going to www.bkconnection.com.

Participate in the Discussion

To see what others are saying about our books and post your own thoughts, check out our blogs at www.bkblogs.com.

Get Quantity Discounts

Berrett-Koehler books are available at quantity discounts for orders of ten or more copies. Please call us toll-free at (800) 929-2929 or email us at bkp.orders@aidcvt.com.

Host a Reading Group

For tips on how to form and carry on a book reading group in your workplace or community, see our website at www.bkconnection.com.

Join the BK Community

Thousands of readers of our books have become part of the "BK Community" by participating in events featuring our authors, reviewing draft manuscripts of forthcoming books, spreading the word about their favorite books, and supporting our publishing program in other ways. If you would like to join the BK Community, please contact us at bkcommunity@bkpub.com.